REASONS TO BE PRETTY

"Mr. LaBute is writing some of the freshest and most illuminating American dialogue to be heard anywhere these days . . . *Reasons* flows with the compelling naturalness of overheard conversation. . . . It's never easy to say what you mean, or to know what you mean to begin with. With a delicacy that belies its crude vocabulary, *Reasons to be Pretty* celebrates the everyday heroism in the struggle to find out." —**Ben Brantley,** *The New York Times*

"[T]here is no doubt that LaBute knows how to hold an audience. . . . LaBute proves just as interesting writing about human decency as when he is writing about the darker urgings of the human heart." —**Charles Spencer,** *Telegraph*

"[F]unny, daring, thought-provoking . . ." —**Sarah Hemming**, *Financial Times*

IN A DARK DARK HOUSE

"Refreshingly reminds us . . . that [LaBute's] talents go beyond glibly vicious storytelling and extend into thoughtful analyses of a world rotten with original sin." —**Ben Brantley,** *The New York Times*

"LaBute takes us to shadowy places we don't like to talk about, sometimes even to think about . . ." —**Erin McClam,** *Newsday*

WRECKS

"Superb and subversive . . . A masterly attempt to shed light on the ways in which we manufacture our own darkness. It offers us the kind of illumination that Tom Stoppard has called 'what's left of God's purpose when you take away God.'" ə *New Yorker*

"[*Wrecks* is a] tasty morse   at has always
informed LaBute's work,   more directly
and urgently than ever he   r, *USA Today*

"*Wrecks* is bound to be identified by its shock value. But it must also be cherished for the moment-by-moment pleasure of its masterly portraiture. There is not an extraneous syllable in LaBute's enormously moving love story." —**Linda Winer,** *Newsday*

FAT PIG

"The most emotionally engaging and unsettling of Mr. LaBute's plays since *bash* . . . A serious step forward for a playwright who has always been most comfortable with judgmental distance." —**Ben Brantley**, *The New York Times*

"One of Neil LaBute's subtler efforts . . . Demonstrates a warmth and compassion for its characters missing in many of LaBute's previous works [and] balances black humor and social commentary in a . . . beautifully written, hilarious . . . dissection of how societal pressures affect relationships [that] is astute and up-to-the-minute relevant." —**Frank Scheck**, *New York Post*

THE MERCY SEAT

"Though set in the cold, gray light of morning in a downtown loft with inescapable views of the vacuum left by the twin towers, *The Mercy Seat* really occurs in one of those feverish nights of the soul in which men and women lock in vicious sexual combat, as in Strindberg's *Dance of Death* and Edward Albee's *Who's Afraid of Virginia Woolf.*" —**Ben Brantley**, *The New York Times*

"[A] powerful drama . . . LaBute shows a true master's hand in gliding us amid the shoals and reefs of a mined relationship." —**Donald Lyons**, *New York Post*

THE SHAPE OF THINGS

"LaBute . . . continues to probe the fascinating dark side of individualism . . . [His] great gift is to live in and to chronicle that murky area of not-knowing, which mankind spends much of its waking life denying." —**John Lahr**, *The New Yorker*

"LaBute is the first dramatist since David Mamet and Sam Shepard—since Edward Albee, actually—to mix sympathy and savagery, pathos and power." —**Donald Lyons**, *New York Post*

"*Shape* . . . is LaBute's thesis on extreme feminine wiles, as well as a disquisition on how far an artist . . . can go in the name of art . . . Like a chiropractor of the soul, LaBute is looking for realignment, listening for a crack." —**John Istel**, *Elle*

BASH

"The three stories in *bash* are correspondingly all, in different ways, about the power instinct, about the animalistic urge for control. In rendering these narratives, Mr. LaBute shows not only a merciless ear for contemporary speech but also a poet's sense of recurring, slyly graduated imagery . . . darkly engrossing." —**Ben Brantley**, *The New York Times*

NEIL LABUTE is an award-winning playwright, filmmaker, and screenwriter. His plays include: *bash*, *The Shape of Things*, *The Distance From Here*, *The Mercy Seat*, *Fat Pig* (Olivier Award nominated for Best Comedy), *Some Girl(s)*, *Reasons to be Pretty* (Tony Award nominated for Best Play), *In A Forest, Dark and Deep*, a new adaptation of *Miss Julie*, and *Reasons to be Happy*. He is the author of *Seconds of Pleasure*, a collection of short fiction, and a 2013 recipient of a Literature Award from the American Academy of Arts and Letters.

Neil LaBute's films include *In the Company of Men* (New York Critics' Circle Award for Best First Feature and the Filmmaker Trophy at the Sundance Film Festival), *Your Friends and Neighbors*, *Nurse Betty*, *Possession*, *The Shape of Things*, *Lakeview Terrace*, *Death at a Funeral*, and *Some Velvet Morning*.

MISS JULIE

MISS JULIE

A PLAY BY
AUGUST STRINDBERG

ADAPTED BY
NEIL LABUTE

THE OVERLOOK PRESS
NEW YORK, NY

First published in paperback in the United States in 2013 by
The Overlook Press, Peter Mayer Publishers, Inc.

141 Wooster Street
New York, NY 10012
www.overlookpress.com
For bulk and special sales, please contact sales@overlookny.com,
or write us at the above address.

Cataloging-in-Publication Data is available from the Library of Congress

Book design and type formatting by Bernard Schleifer
Manufactured in the United States of America
ISBN 978-1-4683-0738-2
10 9 8 7 6 5 4 3 2 1

for the lost generation

"tears gratify a savage nature, they do not melt it . . ."
—PUBLILIUS SYRUS

"all men are bad and in their badness reign . . ."
—WILLIAM SHAKESPEARE

"i'm just a lonely romancer, right at the end of my rope . . ."
—HARRY WARREN & EDGAR LESLIE

PREFACE

How do you solve a problem like *Miss Julie*?

I've stolen that handy little refrain from *The Sound of Music*, but it's a very helpful question when it comes to dealing with such an important, studied and debated play like the one that August Strindberg wrote in his *Miss Julie*. The *problem* that I write of, at least in my mind, is how to take a play that so effortlessly deals with universal and timeless themes and make it your own during the adaptive process (without getting your big muddy paws all over it).

I'm a firm believer in trying things—you may succeed, you may fail, but *trying* is one of the greatest and grandest of ambitions. In the end no one will much care what I've done with this text; it will either work or it won't but the play will live on. Actors will keep scouring it for scenes to perform in class, directors will keep trying to stage it and other playwrights will come along wanting to adapt it in one way or another. That's fine by me and completely expected—"the play's the thing" and this one just happens to be an extraordinarily fine one.

With this text, written in the late 1880s, Strindberg continued to come into his own; to widen and deepen his greatest themes and concerns: love as a currency, the battle of wills that exists between partners (namely men and women) and the power dynamics at the soul of most relationships (be they with colleagues, friends or family). As a writer there would be a number of other ideas that Strindberg tackled on the page but in *Miss Julie* he seemed to be perfectly at home with both his characters and subject—the simplicity with which he uses time, the effortless way he moves his characters about a room, how he allows tragic circumstances to rise up out of the smallest of human gestures. From what I've read Strindberg wasn't a great guy, not the nicest husband or friend or father, but he was a hell of a writer and understood something vast about human frailty (perhaps because he was so frail on so many personal levels himself).

Whatever the case, Strindberg understood people. He may not have loved them or trusted them or always felt comfortable around them, but as a writer he found a way to create them in vivid, beautiful, horrific detail. He dissected the human spirit with the precision of a surgeon and while he genuinely seemed to be frightened (or at least wary) of women and their many gifts and foibles and glories— he was able to write some of modern drama's greatest and most memorable portraits of femininity. Not just Miss Julie but Laura from *The Father* and Tekla from *Creditors* and Eleonora from *Easter* and the wonderful roles (one spoken, one silent) in his play *The Stronger*. Strindberg—in that way that only hugely talented, narcissistic and deeply paranoid geniuses can—even went so far as to accuse his great Norwegian contemporary Henrik Ibsen of stealing from him, as he apparently considered the heroines of both *A Doll's House* and *Hedda Gabler* to be plagiarized versions of what he had already accomplished onstage. How can you not love and admire a guy as simultaneously crazy and talented as that?

Mostly, I just don't care. I love all the scripts I've just mentioned and I go back and read them often. Your career as a playwright begins with your career as a reader. Read everything and read often. Actual books if you can. Feel them in your hands and know that they matter and will matter long after you and I are gone. If you read a play you like, read it again to see why. If you read a play you hate, read it twice more to unlock all the reasons for your displeasure with it. Perhaps you were too hasty (or—gasp!—even wrong) the first time around, but maybe not. Maybe each time will deepen your dislike of it. That's not the point. Know the enemy and how not to do what he or she has done. The best playwriting teachers I've had made me read as much or more than they made me write. Some were annoying (and I suspect not very talented, either) but the ones who pushed me to write and rewrite and read and re-read turned me into a better writer. I've thanked them before but I'll thank them again here for doing what writing teachers should do best: set deadlines, be positive and find the play within the play that each student is trying to write. Do not rewrite it for them or suggest a better ending—any asshole can do that—guide them and nurture them with respect and understanding and love ("tough love" is entirely acceptable but make it the type that any fool can understand).

Adapting Strindberg's pitiless work of three lives in crisis has also made me a better writer. Each moment felt so alive as I worked on it, struggling to find the best word or phrase to underscore what he'd already written while working to make it a part of my own oeuvre as well. It was a great pleasure and a distinct pain in the ass. Painfully slow work, tedious even, but an experience I'm glad to have had and one I'd love to be a part of again. This is not the first play I've adapted (I've also done a version of Georg Büchner's *Woyzeck* and of *Dracula* as well, although that one came straight from the novel and not a dramatic text). The desire to find moments that illuminated the play in some new way for a contemporary audience was intoxicating and carried me through the rough patches when I would barely limp through a page or two a day. A page or two stacks up, however, and soon a version of *Miss Julie* existed with both Strindberg's name and my name on it. I have never collaborated with another writer on a show but in some way it felt as if Strindberg was by my side throughout, offering encouragement, scoffing at some of my ideas but always pushing me on to do good work. I hope I have but that will be for you the reader and future audiences to decide. If he were alive, Strindberg would no doubt take all the credit for this version and I probably wouldn't raise a finger to stop him. A few of my ideas are smart ones, I think, but I just wouldn't be here tackling *Miss Julie* if not for the man himself (every zany, hateful, exuberant inch of him).

I chose to re-set the play in America (on the Long Island Sound in particular) so that the themes of old money and new morals could continue to clash appropriately while resonating in a new way for today's audiences. The world of F. Scott Fitzgerald and his "Jazz Age" is undoubtedly a strong influence here but it goes well beyond the songs and look of the period. I wanted the character of John (Jean in the original version) to be a man who could have tasted the horrors of a world war but also the worldly pleasures of Europe just after the signing of the Armistice. He is a man who hungers for a way of life that he has held briefly in his hands yet works for a rich man whom he both fears and reveres, a man whose estate he has grown up staring at from the dirty window of his own filthy family shack. And the idea of a Miss Julie who is as much a Daisy Buchanan as she is a Swedish aristocrat was not a huge stretch once I began to let my overactive imagination start to get the better of me.

The fatal dance that John and Julie and Kristine enact over the course of a single evening follows the same psychological trajectory of the original text, but as readers and/or viewers today we are constantly aware of the stock market crash that is less than a month away from when these events play out, and the rabbit hole that most of the United States will plunge into almost immediately after. This seemed like a valid and vivid world in which to re-set Strindberg's long night of the soul. I hope it works as an adequately painful playground in your minds if you should read this version, or better yet, see it performed on some local stage, but ultimately you will be the judge of that, although feel free to write my agents rather than me with any and all complaints. I promise to get back to you within a decade.

I've said a lot and yet almost nothing about Strindberg and his marvelous creation. That's a compliment. Like all great works of art, Miss Julie feels intensely familiar and yet remains elusive and mysterious the more time you spend with it.

The world premiere of this version of the play is lucky enough to have a quiet genius at its helm, Jo Bonney, whom I've worked with many times before. It has an amazing cast featuring the gifted Laura Heisler, the darkly charming Logan Marshall-Green and the startlingly beautiful and brilliant Lily Rabe. Sometimes the gods smile down on us.

It also came about because of the good people at the Geffen Playhouse in Westwood (Santa Monica, California), led by the great and gracious Randall Arney. Thank you all for trusting me on this one.

I love this play and I fear it. I know that I will never write anything as good as *Miss Julie* but it's so good that it makes me want to keep trying. I think that's what they call "Art."

Neil LaBute
March 2013

Miss Julie had its American premiere at the Geffen Playhouse in Los Angeles in April 2013. It was directed by Jo Bonney.

JULIE	Lily Rabe
JOHN	Logan Marshall-Green
KRISTINE	Laura Heisler

Silence. Darkness.

Projection #1: "Long Island, N.Y." (Blood red.)
Projection #2: "Labor Day. 1929." (Blood red.)
Projection #3: "Just Before the Crash." (Blood red.)

*Lights up slowly to reveal a kitchen in a palatial estate on the Long
Island Sound. It is obviously a place of work but it maintains some
of the lovely trappings of the stately manor above. A long staircase
leading down into the room.*

*A black and white tiled floor. Archways that lead to many rooms.
Outfitted in every way. Gleaming metal and painted wood. A wall
clock. It's early morning.*

*A massive table in the room with a few chairs and one or two
benches pulled up to it as well. Lilacs in a vase.*

*Gleaming bells attached to a beam of wood over one corner of the
room—captions beneath each one let a person know which room the
sound is coming from.*

*The radio is on. Playing songs from the era. Warm voices fill the air,
backed by sweet music.*

At rise KRISTINE *is standing at the table, chopping up vegetables while keeping one eye on a pan on the stove. She wears an apron over a plain dress. She yawns loudly.*

After a moment JOHN *enters—he is wearing the uniform of a gentleman's valet. A scar on one cheek. A slight limp.*

JOHN *drops a pair of boots on a chair nearby. He throws himself down in another seat and sighs loudly.*

JOHN   . . . she's *crazy* tonight! *Absolutely* mad!

KRISTINE   Oh, so you're finally back, are you?

JOHN   'Course. (*Beat.*) I accompanied *His Majesty* to the station. On the way home I stopped by the dance, just to peek in . . . (*Off* KRISTINE*'s look.*) Not to join 'em, just to look! (*Smiles.*) And there she was, leading the group—dancing with anybody who would have her. The *second* she saw me she came rushing over and asked me to save a song for her. When we finally danced you've never seen anything like it, the way we—she's out of her mind again, I swear it!

KRISTINE   I'm not surprised . . . she's been worse than ever these last few weeks. (*Thinks.*) Well, at least since her engagement ended . . .

JOHN   Ha! What a *fiasco* that turned out to be! (*Stands.*) And a pretty decent fellow, too. Not much of a *fortune*, from what I hear, but still . . . (*Beat.*) Why do you suppose she'd want to stay here with us, instead of going off with her father to visit those cousins of hers . . . ?

He doesn't wait for an answer but instead rises up, going to a cupboard and producing a shoeshine box. Polish and waxes and rags.

KRISTINE I'll bet she's afraid to face them . . . after all that happened with her young man.

He hovers for a minute near KRISTINE, *even though (for the moment at least) she is having none of it and keeps busy with her work.*

JOHN No doubt! (*Beat.*) Did you ever hear that whole story, what went on between them, the last time? (*Smiles.*) I saw the *whole* thing . . . even though I had to pretend not to notice.

KRISTINE Wait . . . you *saw* it?

JOHN I absolutely did. They were down by the stables and she was—get this—"training him," as she called it. You know what she was doing? She was making him jump over a riding crop. (*Off* KRISTINE*'s look.*) She was! He jumped over it twice . . . and both times she smacked him with it as he went by. The third time, he pulled it out of her hand, snapped it across his knee— (*He mimes this.*)—just like that! SNAP! Then he hit her with it, across the face . . . he threw it aside and stormed off.

KRISTINE Did he *really*? I can't believe it!

JOHN He did, though . . . and so that was the end of that. (*Looks around.*) You got anything there for me to eat, sweetie?

She points toward a plate on a counter. A little mound of food on a plate.

KRISTINE . . . just that bit of kidney. I cut it off and put it aside for you.

JOHN That was nice of—(*Goes to it.*) Well, you could've at *least* covered it for me.

KRISTINE Ha! You're worse than *His Majesty* . . . (*She tugs at his hair playfully.*) Silly.

JOHN Hey, hey, stop that now! Don't get me all riled up . . . (*Smiles.*)
You know what that leads to.

KRISTINE Oh, hush! I was just being playful . . .

JOHN *grabs her and they play with each other for a moment until*
KRISTINE *escapes.* JOHN *takes his plate to the table and sits.*

KRISTINE *brings a beer and puts it down next to him.* JOHN *looks at it.*
Displeased. He begrudgingly eats part of the meal.

JOHN A *beer*? On the last day of summer? No thanks, I can have
that anytime . . . give me something better!

JOHN *jumps up, goes to a cabinet and pulls out a bottle of wine.*
A fancy label on it.

JOHN Here! See? And look at that seal . . . all done up in gold! Get
me a glass, love—one of those *real* wine glasses—I want things to
be just right tonight!

KRISTINE (*As she gets a glass.*) God help the woman who gets you
for a husband! I've never seen such a fuss!

JOHN Stop now . . . you'd be happy to have me as your husband,
I know that much! Hasn't hurt your reputation for people to see
you as my sweetheart. (*Tastes the wine.*) Mmmmm. Nice. Very
nice. Could be just a touch warmer. (*To* KRISTINE.) He got this in
Dijon—overpaid for it—and shipping and taxes, too. (*Stops, sniffs
the air.*) What're you cooking in there? That smells awful . . .

JOHN *tops off his glass of wine and finishes it. He then picks up the
boots and goes to a nearby bench. Starts his polishing regimen.*

KRISTINE Oh . . . it's just some damn *potion* that Miss Julie is demanding for Diana.

JOHN Better watch your language there! (*Grins.*) Anyway, why're you cooking for that bitch of hers . . . *and* on a holiday! Is she sick?

KRISTINE I should say so! (*Beat.*) She got out and was running around with that mutt that the groundskeeper has . . . (*Quietly.*) Now she's gotten herself into trouble. Miss Julie's beside herself but doesn't know what to do about it . . . *of course* . . .

JOHN Our "little miss" is too prideful about some things and not enough about others. Just like her mother, when she was alive! *That* one was more at home in the kitchen and the stables than anywhere else . . . and yet nothing was ever good enough for her. Her cuffs were always dirty, but each of her buttons had a *coat of arms* on 'em . . . (*Beat.*) And now here's her daughter . . . she doesn't have any respect for her clothes, either. Or *herself*, for that matter. If I *ever* let my uniform get that way—not just now, but in the service, too—doesn't matter. She's got no grace, if you want my opinion. (*Beat.*) . . . out in the barn just now, she snatched that chauffeur away from Anna and forced him to dance with her . . . *we'd* never do that!! But that's what happens when these folks try to act like common people. They *become* common! I mean, she's a nice-looking girl . . . don't get me wrong. Beautiful figure . . . (*Noticing* KRISTINE.) . . . and so on. Nice *shoulders*.

KRISTINE Don't get too carried away—Clara dresses her and you should hear some of the things she has to say about her . . .

JOHN *Clara*? Ha! Women are always jealous! *I've* watched her out riding before . . . and seen the way she dances!

KRISTINE *moves closer to* JOHN. *Trying another tactic with him.*

KRISTINE Will you dance with *me* tonight? John? I mean, when
  I'm finished here . . .

JOHN Of course I will.

KRISTINE *sits down next to him. Only a few inches away.*

KRISTINE Promise?

JOHN *Promise?* Look, when I say I'll do a thing then I do it . . .
  (*He turns to her.*) Thanks for supper, by the way . . . it was good.

*They begin to have a moment. Not kissing yet but touching and
getting closer. And closer.*

And now she arrives. Miss Julie. By voice before we see her:

JULIE (*O.S.*) . . . no, don't wait! I'll be right back!

In unison KRISTINE *and* JOHN *move apart.* KRISTINE *picks up something
from a counter and moves back toward her duties while* JOHN *slips
over to the table. He corks the wine and places it into a cabinet.
Clears the wine glass as well.*

He then returns to his work on the boots. Cleaning them.

Finally JULIE *appears. In white from head to toe. Sequins and beads.
Breathtaking in the way that some people just are: merely by existing.*

JULIE *notices* KRISTINE *first, calling out to her without moving down
the stairs.*

JULIE Well? Is it ready yet?

KRISTINE *doesn't speak but indicates that* JOHN *is in the room. He nods
to* JULIE *and steps away from his work.*

JOHN I can leave if you ladies have secrets to discuss . . .

JULIE *smiles and moves down into the kitchen. She flicks her handkerchief playfully at his face.*

JULIE It's certainly none of your business . . . if that's what you mean. (*Beat.*) Curious?

JOHN (*Sniffing.*) *Violets* . . . I like that . . .

JULIE Shame on you! (*Smiles.*) So you know all about perfumes, too, do you? Well, you certainly have your charms, I'll give you that.

JULIE *has been backing toward* KRISTINE *while* JOHN *presses in on her. Before he can get any closer, she puts up her hand. Stopping him from going deeper into the kitchen.*

JULIE Ah, ah! Go away now . . . no peeking!

JOHN I suppose it's some sort of witch's brew that *ladies* cook up on a night like this. A little something to help them see their futures—or at least a glimpse of their *future* husbands!

JULIE Ha! Well . . . you'll need *very* good eyes to see that, if you're meaning "me!"

JULIE *defiantly lets this statement hang in the air.* JOHN *finally nods and looks away. Nothing to say in return.*

After a moment, JULIE *turns to* KRISTINE. *More demanding:*

JULIE Pour it into a bottle and cork it for me. (*To* JOHN.) Come and dance while I wait for her to finish . . .

JOHN Not to be rude, Miss, but I've promised my next dance to Kristine.

JULIE Oh, she can always dance with you later! A different time . . . (*To* KRISTINE.) You'll lend him to me, won't you, Kristine?

KRISTINE It's not up to me, Miss. (*To* JOHN.) If the Mistress is kind enough to invite you to dance, then you shouldn't say *no* to her. Go on, and be sure to thank her for the *honor* . . .

JOHN To be honest—and I don't mean to cause any offense—but is it right for you to dance with the same partner twice in an evening? I mean, with the way people are so quick to talk around here?

JULIE Why? Whatever would they have to talk about? I don't get your point.

JOHN Well, if you refuse to understand then I'll have to speak more clearly. Spell it out for you. (*Beat.*) Many of your servants are expecting the same honor tonight, so it hardly seems fair to single me out . . .

JULIE Ha! "Single you out!" How ridiculous. I'm a little amazed, frankly. (*Beat.*) I am the Mistress of this estate and I thought I was being *courteous* to my servants by attending their dance, and if I'm going to do that, then I want to be with someone who can dance as well as I can so I don't look foolish. (*Beat.*) Understood?

JOHN *weighs this before speaking. A glance at* KRISTINE.

JOHN Fine. At your service, Miss.

JULIE No, don't say it like that! Tonight's a holiday. We're celebrating. Right now we're just people. Happy people enjoying ourselves . . . I don't want to think about "rank" or "status" or "place." (*To* JOHN.) Just give me your arm. (*To* KRISTINE.) And don't fret, Kristine . . . I won't steal away with your *partner*! Nor for long, anyway!

JOHN *looks over at* KRISTINE *one more time, then puts out his arm for* JULIE. *She takes it and out they go together. Up the stairs and off into the night.*

KRISTINE *stands frozen for a moment, watching them leave. After a bit, she crosses to the radio and fiddles with the tuner. Changing stations. Another song plays softly.*

She returns to her duties, first putting the concoction on the stove into a bottle and corking it.

KRISTINE *sets this aside and then begins to clean up after* JOHN. *Removes his plate and glass to the sink. She washes each and sets them aside. Stopping to listen to the music from time to time. Sways to a song as if she were dancing.*

When she's finished, she takes off her apron, looking at the kitchen to make sure that it's being left tidy.

KRISTINE *crosses to a drawer, pulls out a comb and mirror and goes to the table. Props up the mirror on the vase of lilacs and begins to play with her hair. Tries to give it some curl (after the fashion of the day).*

She yawns and checks the time on the clock. Sitting for a minute, KRISTINE *notices the handkerchief (that* JULIE *was carrying) on the table. It's been left behind.*

She suddenly stands and crosses to it—with precision and instinct, KRISTINE *folds it in half and then in quarters. She looks around, then smells it. Closes her eyes as she takes in a whiff of violets.*

A moment later and JOHN *returns. Jaunty and whistling, he moves down the kitchen steps and smiles at* KRISTINE.

JOHN   God, that girl . . . the way she moves! It's completely crazy!
(*He imitates the Charleston.*) They were laughing at her—at *us*—
behind our backs. (*Beat.*) Can you believe that? Hmm?

*He picks up the bottle that she has prepared and studies it for a bit.
Sets it down.*

KRISTINE   . . . well, she always gets that way when . . . never
mind. (*Looks at* JOHN.) Will you dance with *me* soon, John?
Finally?

JOHN   You're not mad at me, are you? For going off like that?

KRISTINE   No, I'm not . . . not for a little thing like that. Why, should
I be? (*Beat.*) Besides, I know *my* place . . .

JOHN   Ahhh, you're a sensible girl, Kristine . . .

JOHN *goes to her, slowly slips an arm around her. Pulling her close.
They begin to move together, to the music from the radio. Dancing.
Touching.*

JOHN   . . . you'll make someone a good wife one day.

KRISTINE *puts her head on* JOHN'*s shoulder and they dance to the slow
song that is coming from the speakers.*

JULIE *enters and stops on the steps. Watches the two of them for
a moment.*

*She is not pleased but she catches herself. Waits. Forces herself to
be good-humored as she finally does interrupt them:*

JULIE . . . you're not much of an *escort*, are you? Running off on
your partner like that . . .

JOHN On the contrary, Miss, you can see that I came running back
to the partner that I'd deserted.

JULIE *starts to argue but stops. Concedes the point. She moves
further into the room while* JOHN *and* KRISTINE *break apart. They stand
awkwardly waiting, unsure how to react.*

JULIE You know, there's no one here who can dance like you do.
No one. (*Looking at him.*) But why're you still in uniform? *And* on
a holiday! Go change at once . . .

JOHN Alright, but I'll have to ask you to leave for a moment. (*Points.*)
My best coat's on that hook over there . . .

JOHN *points off, toward his own room.* JULIE *follows his finger and
shakes her head.*

JULIE Ha! Are you actually worried about taking off your *coat* with
me in the room? (*Beat.*) Fine. Then go inside and do it, or stay
here and I'll turn around.

JOHN Very well. With your permission . . .

JOHN *moves off and just out of sight. We can catch just a glimpse of
him as he changes clothing.*

JULIE *waits, finally turning her attentions to* KRISTINE.

JULIE Tell me, Kristine, you and John seem very familiar with each
other . . . what are you, "sweethearts?" Or more? (*Beat.*) *Engaged*?

KRISTINE I'm not sure, Miss. We like to call it that. After all, you
  yourself were . . .

JULIE Yes, but I was *properly* engaged.

KRISTINE Still. It didn't come to anything, did it? In the end,
  I mean . . .

Before JULIE *can say anything in return* JOHN *enters. He is dressed in
a smart suit jacket (after the fashion of the day).*

JULIE *Très gentil, Monsieur Jean. Très gentil.*

JOHN *Vous voulez plaisanter, Madame.*

JULIE *Et vous voulez parler français!* (*Smiling.*) Where did you learn
  to speak like that?

JOHN During the war. (*Beat.*) And after.

A moment hangs over all of them. JULIE *nods, taking in this information.*
KRISTINE *waits. Finally,* JOHN *helps to move the conversation forward
by saying:*

JOHN I was a wine steward in one of the best hotels in Lucerne.
  Learned my trade.

JULIE Well, you look like quite the gentleman in that outfit.
  Charmant!

JOHN . . . I'm sure you're just flattering me.

JULIE "Flattering you!" Ha! Why should I?

JOHN Well, my natural modesty and position in this household
  forbid me from presuming that you're actually *complimenting*
  me, so I am taking the liberty of assuming that you're *exaggerating*
  —or what some people might politely call *flattery*.

JULIE   My goodness . . . wherever did you learn to talk like *that*?! You must've spent many evenings at the *theater*!

JOHN   I have. Been a fair few times. *And* I've traveled to places as well . . .

JULIE   But you're from around here, aren't you?

JOHN   I am. My father was a groundsman on the estate next to yours . . . (*Beat.*) I saw you many times when you were little, but you never noticed me, of course.

JULIE   No! *Really*?

JOHN   Oh yes. I remember one time—nothing. I can't tell you about that right now.

JULIE   *What*? No, don't be like that . . . of *course* you can say it.

JOHN   . . . some other time perhaps . . .

JULIE   Which means you'll never tell me. What's the harm in saying it now?

JOHN   No harm, I'd just rather not, if it's all the same to you . . .

JOHN *stops, not wishing to go any further.* JULIE *keeps looking at him, pressing in. Uncomfortable,* JOHN *looks over at* KRISTINE *(who in the meantime has sat down in a kitchen chair and fallen asleep).*

JOHN   Ahh, look. Poor thing.

JULIE   Ha! She'll make someone a lovely wife, I'm sure . . . I'll bet she even *snores*.

JOHN   No, she doesn't. (*Beat.*) But she talks in her sleep.

JULIE   Oh? (*Studying him.*) And how would you know *that*?

JOHN   (*Coolly.*) I've seen her.

JULIE *decides to let this pass—she moves to the table and sits. Indicates for* JOHN *to join her.*

JULIE Won't you sit down?

JOHN I'm sorry, Miss, but I couldn't. I won't be so bold, not in your presence.

JULIE And what if I *ordered* you?

JOHN Then I'd obey.

JULIE Then please do. (*Thinking.*) Wait, could you get me something to drink first?

JOHN Of course. I'm not sure what's left in the icebox. Only beer, I'm afraid.

JULIE That's fine with me . . . *more* than fine. I prefer it to wine, actually. I have very simple tastes.

JOHN *goes to the icebox and retrieves* JULIE *a bottle of beer. Brings it to her on a plate and with a glass. He opens it for her.*

JOHN At your service.

JULIE Thank you! (*Waits.*) Will you join me?

JOHN I'm not partial to beer, actually.

JULIE I see. So does that make you the kind of man who allows a woman to drink alone then?

JOHN That's a very good point. Forgive me.

JOHN *goes over and gets another bottle and a glass. He checks on* KRISTINE *as he passes her—she's still asleep.*

JOHN *returns and opens his bottle. Pours out a glassful.*

JULIE   Drink to my health! (*Waits.*) What, are you shy?

JOHN *checks to make sure that* KRISTINE *is still asleep then takes his glass, kneels in a "romantic" way while he toasts* JULIE.

JOHN   To your health, good lady!

JULIE   Bravo! Now kiss my foot and all will be forgiven.

She holds out her foot. JOHN *hesitates but then moves to her. He boldly takes hold of her shoe and lightly kisses it.* JULIE *claps.*

JULIE   Excellent! You should've been an actor!

JOHN   (*Rising up.*) Alright . . . this ought to stop now, Miss. Anyone could walk in and see us . . . or if Kristine happened to wake up . . .

JULIE   *And?*

JOHN   *And* people would talk, that's what. You have no idea how many tongues were going out there earlier, *wagging* themselves to death!

JULIE   What were they saying? Tell me. (*Patting the table.*) *Sit* down.

JOHN   (*Sitting.*) I don't want to be insensitive to you but some unkind things were being said—*awful* things—coarse things that I'm sure you can imagine for yourself pretty easily. You're not *that* innocent . . . and when a woman is seen drinking with a man—and her own *servant* at that—well . . . that's . . .

JULIE   "Well" what? *What?* (*Beat.*) Anyway, it's not as if we're on our own. Kristine is here.

JOHN   Yes, but she's *asleep!*

JULIE   Then I'll wake her up! (*Going to her.*) Are you asleep, Kristine? Wake up!

JULIE *shakes* KRISTINE *by the shoulder. Nothing happens.*

JULIE She certainly sleeps soundly! (*Grabbing Kristine's nose.*)
. . . wake up now! Come on!

JOHN (*Standing up.*) STOP IT!

JULIE *stops what she's doing. Turns slowly to face* JOHN. *A moment passes between them.*

JOHN Let her sleep.

JULIE *Why*?

JOHN She has a right to be tired . . . standing over a hot stove all day. People should be respected. In their *sleep*, anyway.

JULIE (*Moving away from* KRISTINE.) What a kind thought! It does you credit. And you're right, of course . . . thank you.

JULIE *has moved to the base of the stairs. She looks as if she might be leaving but she suddenly turns to* JOHN. *Holds out her hand to him.*

JULIE . . . come outside and pick me some lilacs.

Before JOHN *can answer* KRISTINE *stirs.* JULIE *stays up against the wall and* JOHN *moves aside and just out of sight.*

KRISTINE *doesn't fully wake, dropping back off to sleep.* JULIE *and* JOHN *move away from her. Speaking quietly:*

JULIE (*Whispering.*) *Please* come?

JOHN Outside again? *With* you?

JULIE Yes.

JOHN No, we can't do that! Absolutely not!

JULIE Why not? (*Beat.*) Surely you don't think . . .

JOHN   No, not me . . . but the others might.

JULIE   What? That I'm in *love* with my servant?

JOHN   I'm not conceited, Miss, but it's been known to happen . . . and nothing is sacred to those people out there . . . (*He points.*) I can't. I *won't.*

JULIE   Well, well . . . sounds like you're moving up in the world.

JOHN   Yes, I am. *Trying* to.

JULIE   Just as I'm coming down . . .

JOHN   Take my advice, Miss, *don't* come down—no one'll ever believe you came down on your own. They'll all say you *fell.*

JULIE   Seems like *I* have a much higher opinion of people than you do. (*Offers her hand again.*) Come with me . . . let's go find out who's right.

JOHN   (*Studying her.*) You're a very strange person, Miss. Do you know that?

JULIE *nods at this and leans back against the wall of the kitchen. Drifting to the sound of the radio.*

JULIE   Maybe I am but so are you . . . in fact, the whole world is strange. Animals, people. All of it. It's all scum . . . floating on the water and then sinking. Sinking . . . (*Beat.*) That reminds me of a dream I've had: I'm sitting on a pillar but I don't see a way to get down. Each time I glance down my head starts to spin—I *want* to get down—but I don't have the courage to jump off . . . I can't hold on any longer, I need to fall . . . but I don't. I know that I'll never feel safe until I find my way down, down to the ground . . . and if I do get there, I'll want to crawl underground. *Deep* into it. (*Beat.*) Have you ever felt like that?

JOHN   No. The opposite for me. I dream I'm in a forest lying under a tree. I need to get up there—I *have* to—up to the top to look down on the world below me and to steal the eggs, those *golden* eggs, from the bird's nest hidden in the branches. I try to find my way up, I keep climbing and climbing, but the tree is so big and the bark is so smooth—even to reach the first branch seems impossible—but I know that if I can get there I'll go up the rest like it was a *ladder!* I haven't made it yet but I'm sure I will some-day . . . (*Beat.*) Even if it's only a dream.

JULIE *smiles and once again offers her hand to* JOHN.

JULIE Here we are talking about *dreams* . . . when we could go out onto the grounds!! Come on!!

Finally JOHN *goes to her, taking her hand and holding it close to his face.*

JOHN We'll need to sleep with flowers under our pillows tonight so our dreams will come true!

They start up the steps but almost immediately he stops; JOHN *puts a hand up to one eye.*

JULIE Did you get something in your eye? Here. Let me see.
JOHN It's alright—a bit of dirt, that's all—it'll be gone soon.
JULIE No, just—it must've been from my sleeve when I brushed up against you.

She looks around, noticing her handkerchief on the table.

JULIE *points in that direction and leads* JOHN *back into the room. Sitting him down at the table.*

JULIE Sit over here. Let me help you. (*Takes the handkerchief and tries to dab it in the corner of his eye.*) Now, don't move! Just sit still. (*Slaps his hand.*) Didn't you *hear* what I said? (*Waits.*) See? Now you're trembling, a big strong man like you . . . (*Feels his biceps.*) And such arms!

JOHN Please, Miss!

JULIE What is it, *Monsieur Jean*?

JOHN *Attention; je ne suis qu'un homme!*

JULIE Just be still! (*Checks.*) There. Now it's gone. (*Puts her hand out.*) Kiss my hand and thank me . . .

JOHN Wait, Miss, *listen*! (*Getting up.*) Kristine is right *there* . . . (*Points.*) . . . so will you *please* listen to me . . .

JULIE Kiss my hand first.

JOHN LISTEN! (*Beat.*) It's very late, Miss . . .

JULIE Kiss my hand *first*.

JOHN Alright . . . but you've only got yourself to blame now . . .

JULIE For what?

JOHN You're twenty-five! You're *not* a child! It's dangerous when you play with *fire* . . .

JULIE Not for me. I'm *insured*.

JOHN No, you're not! And even if you are, it's still—there is highly flammable material here. (*Beat.*) Don't you understand?

JULIE Meaning "you?"

JOHN Yes, and not just because it's "me" but because I'm a young man . . . and . . . I'm . . .

JULIE *What*? Highly seductive . . . and handsome . . . how terribly conceited! A *Don Juan*, would you say? Yes, that's it! You're *Don Juan*.

JOHN Am I?

JULIE Good Heavens, I'm *terrified* . . .

JULIE *tries to appear strong but* JOHN *has backed her up against the table. Suddenly he is holding her. He pulls her close and kisses her.*

Almost immediately she moves away from him but first she smacks her palm against the side of his face.

JULIE Stop it! Don't touch me.

JOHN (*Uncertain.*) . . . is that serious or joking?

JULIE I'm being serious.

JOHN Then you're very dangerous, Miss, because I can't tell what's for real and what isn't. (*Yawns.*) Besides, it's too late to play with you now . . . so if you'll forgive me I'll get back to what I was doing. Your father likes his things ready for riding . . . and it's nearly morning now. Excuse me.

Without waiting for an answer JOHN *walks away from* JULIE *and returns to the boots. Sits and begins to clean them.* JULIE *watches him for a moment, then speaks:*

JULIE (*Firmly.*) . . . put those boots down.

JOHN Sorry, Miss, it's part of my job. I don't have a *choice* . . . but I do about being your *plaything* and I choose not to and I never will.

JULIE Aren't *we* the "proud" one?

JOHN In some ways—not in others.

JULIE (*Changing tack.*) . . . and have you ever been in love?

JOHN We don't use that word but yes, I've been *fond* of lots of girls—and a few women—I even got sick once because I couldn't get the one I wanted. *Sick.* Do you know what I mean? Like those princes in *The Arabian Nights* who can't eat or drink because of love. That was me.

JULIE   *And*? (*Waits.*) Who was she?

JOHN   You can't force me to answer that.

JULIE   But if I asked you as an equal—as your "friend"—who was she?

JOHN   You.

JOHN *said this matter-of-factly. Why not? It's the truth.* JULIE *stares at him without speaking. This catches her by surprise: a girl who usually likes to do the surprising.*

JOHN *calmly removes his best jacket and replaces it. He returns in his shirt and trousers with braces. Rolls up his sleeves and sits.*

JULIE *sits and doesn't say anything for a moment. Watches as* JOHN *continues to clean her father's boots.*

JULIE   . . . how silly.

JOHN   Yes! I suppose it is. *Ridiculous*, even . . . that's why I didn't want to tell you the story before. But I will now. (*Beat.*) I wonder if you can imagine what the world looks like from down below? No, you can't . . . *how* could you? It's like the hawks and falcons overhead . . . we never see their backs because they're always up there, hovering above us. Out of reach. (*Beat.*) I grew up in a small house, a *shack* . . . with seven brothers and sisters and a pig. In the middle of a wasteland, a *valley of ashes*, without even a single tree. Just over there. (*Pointing.*) But from our uppermost window we could see the wall of your father's garden with just the tops of the apple trees that were sticking up into the sky . . .

to me it was like a Garden of Eden, guarded by angry angels with flaming swords . . . Nevertheless, some other boys and myself found our way in. To the tree of life. (*Waits.*) Do you find that contemptible?

JULIE Stealing apples? No, not at all. Boys do that kind of thing . . .

JOHN That's what you say now, but you still think I'm a thief. (*Beat.*) Nonetheless, I got into that paradise again one day: I went there with my mother to help weed the onion patch. Next to the vegetable beds there was a Turkish pavilion that was shaded by jasmine trees and covered in honeysuckle. I couldn't *imagine* what it was used for, but I'd never seen such a beautiful thing. People would go in and out of it, all day long. In and out. Then one time, the door was left open. I went inside—I *sneaked* in— pictures of kings and emperors covered the walls and red velvet curtains with *tassels* hung over the windows. (*Looking at her.*) You know what I'm talking about, don't you? The *outhouse*.

JOHN *snaps a sprig of lilac from the arrangement on the table. Hands it to* JULIE, *who puts it up to her nose.*

JOHN I'd never even been inside *this* house, never been anywhere other than *church,* but this was the most beautiful place I'd ever seen, and no matter what I'd think about, my thoughts would always come back to it. That place. Gradually, I was overcome by a desire to experience it, the *full* pleasure of it . . . until one day, I did. I snuck inside, sat down . . . looked around. *Marveled* at its beauty. And just then, I heard someone coming. I had to get out! There's only one way out for you folks—the upper class—but *I* had to find another way out, a lower way . . . I lifted the lid and I found it; and then I *took* it. (*Beat.*) Afterwards, I ran away, ran

like mad . . . through the raspberry bushes and strawberry fields,
all the way to a rose terrace. And there I caught a glimpse of a
pink dress and white stockings. *You.* I crawled into the weeds—
with thorns that were pricking me and through the filth—so that
I could watch you. *Look* at you. Walking amongst the roses.
And I thought to myself, "If it's true that a thief can enter the
Kingdom of Heaven and be with the angels . . . how strange it is
that this poor man's son isn't allowed into a rose garden to play
with a rich man's child."

JULIE *places her hand on top of* JOHN's. *He looks over at her. Silence
for a moment.*

JULIE . . . do you think all poor children feel that way?

JOHN "Do all poor . . . " Yes! Of *course* they do!

JULIE It must be horrible to be poor.

JOHN Oh . . . Miss . . . you have *no* idea! A dog can lie on the
sofa with its mistress and a horse can have its nose patted by
a young lady's hand, but a servant . . . (*He stops.*) Of course
there's exceptions now and then . . . someone *brave* enough
to make his own way in the world—but not very often.

JOHN *carefully removes his hand from* JULIE's. *He sits back and
finishes his story:*

JOHN Anyway, do you know what I did after I saw you? I jumped
into the stream, got found and pulled out of the water and beaten.
But the following Sunday . . . when my family went off to visit a
relative, I was able to stay behind. I cleaned myself with soap and
water and put on my best shirt and went to church . . . just so

I could see you *one* more time. And I did. I saw you. When I
went back I was ready to die, but quietly, perfectly, without any
pain to it. I remembered that it was dangerous for a person to
sleep under an elder bush and we had one in full bloom. I tore
off every leaf, every budding flower, and I made a little bed of it in
the oat bin . . . in the barn. Have you ever noticed how soft oats
are? *So* soft to the human skin . . . (*Thinking.*) I closed down the
lid, shut my eyes and drifted off to sleep. When I awoke I was
very sick but I didn't die . . . as you can see. *What* did I hope to
prove by doing all that? I have no idea. Maybe because there
was no way to have you—it symbolized the hopelessness of
never being able to get out of the life that I was born into. (*Beat.*)
Maybe.

JULIE (*Sincerely.*) . . . you have a lovely way with words. Did you
ever go to school?

JOHN Some, and I've read a lot of novels and seen a few plays.
I've also listened to other people talk, *cultured* people. *That* taught
me the most.

JULIE You mean you stand around listening to what we have to say?
Our *conversations*?

JOHN Of course! And I've heard an earful, too, from the front seat of
the car or rowing your boats. One time, you and your girlfriend
were talking . . . and . . .

JULIE *Yes*? What was it you think you heard?

JOHN I don't want to say, but I will say this: I was certainly amazed
. . . wondering where you might've learned such *language*! Maybe
in the end, there really isn't that much difference between people
. . . at least not as much as we think.

JULIE Nonsense! That's not true! The people in my world don't
behave like you people do when we're engaged . . .

JOHN Are you *sure*? (*Beat.*) Come now, Miss, you don't have to play "innocent" with me . . .

JULIE The man I gave my love to was a cad. He was a shit.

JOHN That's what you *all* say—afterwards.

JULIE "All?"

JOHN I've heard *those* phrases used before, anyhow. On similar occasions.

JULIE What occasions?

JOHN The one we just spoke of, for instance . . . before. You and that girlfriend of yours.

JULIE Alright, just stop! (*Beat.*) I don't want to hear any more about this . . .

JOHN That's interesting. Neither did she, if I remember correctly. (*Yawns.*) Well, I think I'll be off to bed, if you'll excuse me.

JOHN *makes this proclamation but doesn't move until* JULIE *allows it. She waits, thinking what to say. Finally:*

JULIE To *bed*? It's almost daylight!

JOHN Yes, but going back and dancing with those fools out there doesn't really interest me . . . and it's very late.

JULIE (*Suggestively.*) . . . then get the keys to the boathouse and row me out onto the water . . . I want to see the sunrise.

She makes a slight move toward JOHN *and he does the same toward her. They stop, hovering in that space just before an embrace.*

JOHN Do you think that's wise, Miss?

JULIE Are you worried about your *reputation*?

JOHN Why shouldn't I be? Laughed at or even worse—*sacked*—

just when I'm trying to get ahead in this world. Besides, I've got
a certain obligation to Kristine . . .

JULIE Ah! So it's "Kristine" now, is it?

JOHN Yes, but this is for you, too. Listen to me and go upstairs . . .
go to bed.

JULIE Ha! So now I take orders from *you*?

JOHN Just this once, for your *own* sake! It's late, you're tired and
a little drunk . . . you don't know what you're doing here. Go to
bed. *Please.* (*Beat.*) If the others come looking for me and find us
here . . . you're lost. Do you hear me? *Lost.* Not me. *You.*

JOHN *doesn't wait any longer—he goes to the table and clears the
plates and glasses.* JULIE *watches him as he works. He leaves the
two bottles where they are.*

She moves to the radio. Swaying to the music it plays.

JULIE I know these people and I love them just as much as they
love me. Let them come . . . you'll see.

JOHN "Love" you? They don't *love* you! They may take your
food, but they *spit* on it! It's the *truth*, Miss, believe me! You
have *no* idea what they're saying about you . . . and you'd
better never listen!

JULIE (*Surprised.*) What do they say?

JOHN Nasty things . . . about you . . . and now *me*, too. (*Going to
her.*) *Please*, Miss! GO!

JULIE Cowards!

JOHN Mobs are always cowardly but you can't fight them, all you
can do is run . . .

JOHN *holds her but instead of moving away she kisses him. Just a peck at first but it grows into something deeper. He tries to stop himself but now it's too late.*

She pulls away at first, but then puts her head on his shoulder. JOHN *holds her tightly against his body.*

JULIE I can't run away from you . . . (*Looking around.*) Where should we go? Not in there . . . that's Kristine's room . . .

JOHN Yes, but over there's my room.

JULIE *pulls away, looking at him.* JOHN *holds onto her and speaks directly to her. Looking deep into her eyes.*

JOHN We can't bother with conventions now . . . and you can trust me, Miss. I promise. I'm your friend. Your true and respectful friend . . .

JULIE . . . but . . . what if someone *does* come looking for you? (*Toward* KRISTINE.) What about . . . ?

JOHN I'll bolt the door. If anyone beats on it or breaks it down, then I'll *kill* them . . . for you. (*Begging her.*) Please! Come with me!

JULIE . . . do you promise . . . ?

JULIE *hesitates and* JOHN *kisses her. This time she does not fight him but melts into his arms. She pulls at his shirt and he works to unbutton her dress. They kiss and tear at each other as his hands disappear inside of her dress. They move slowly toward the door of his room.*

JOHN *turns the radio up even louder on the way—music of the period floods into the room. They disappear into the shadows of his doorway.*

Only the two bottles and JULIE*'s purse are sitting on the table now. Light is beginning to shine in from a window nearby. The sound of* JOHN *and* JULIE *in the distance. Making love.*

After a while, KRISTINE *wakes up. Looks around. Noticing that the radio is still on, she goes to turn it off when she sees the bottles and suddenly stops. Notices* JULIE*'s purse as well.*

More sounds from JOHN*'s room. She listens.*

KRISTINE *turns toward* JOHN*'s bedroom and goes to it. She listens more intently. Her eyes tell us the whole story. She brushes away a tear.*

KRISTINE *goes to turn down the radio but stops herself.*

She stands for a beat, unsure what to do next. Finally, she exits slowly back to her room.

The kitchen is empty once again except for the sound of the radio and the lovers offstage.

Another moment passes and JULIE *enters. Goes to her purse on the table and checks her make-up. Puts powder on her nose with a puff.*

JOHN *enters a beat later, in his undershirt and braces on his trousers pulled up over his shoulders. He seems to be excited. Agitated. Alive. He goes to* JULIE *and pulls her close, dancing a few slow steps with her. Embracing her.*

JOHN . . . we can't possibly stay here now. You know that, don't you?

JULIE Yes, but where can we go?

JOHN Leave here. Travel. As far as we can go.

JULIE Yes, but *where*?

JOHN *suddenly notices that* KRISTINE *is no longer asleep in the chair. He moves over toward her door. Listening. He seems satisfied but wary.*

JULIE *notices this behavior but appears less concerned (for now).*

JOHN . . . maybe Switzerland. The Italian lakes. (*Beat.*) Have you ever been there?

JULIE No. Is it beautiful?

JOHN Ah! It's an eternal summer there! Oranges and laurel trees! It's wonderful . . .

JULIE But what'll we do there?

JOHN I'll open a hotel—a first-class place for first-class customers.

JULIE A *hotel*?

JOHN Yes! *That's* the life! Always new faces, new languages . . . and your work is right there in front of you, day and night. Bells ringing, train whistles blowing, people coming and going all the time, and the money pouring in. *Flooding* us. That's the life *I* want!

JULIE Fine, that's what you want . . . but what about me?

JOHN *You*? You'll be the mistress of it all! The absolute jewel in the crown!! . . . with those looks of yours, our success will be guaranteed! You can sit in the office all day like a queen, with your slaves running around with just a push of an electric button!

Our guests will file past your throne and leave their offerings at
your feet! At your *feet*!

JOHN *has worked himself up with the vision of this—he pulls* JULIE
to a bench and sits her down.

JOHN You have *no* idea how they'll cower when they're presented
with their bill!! How much they'll tremble! (*Smiles.*) I'll pour *salt*
on their bills and then you can add the *sugar* on top with your
pretty smile! (*He stands, offers his hand.*) Come on, we should
leave now, as soon as we can. I've got a timetable for the trains
here . . . and if we can book passage . . . then . . .

JOHN *goes to a drawer, rummaging around for a timetable.*

JULIE That all sounds fine, John . . . it sounds wonderful but first you
have to give me strength! Come put your arms around me, tell me
you love me! (*Beat.*) *Please* do it!

JOHN *has stopped what he's doing and glances back at* KRISTINE'S
room. He turns back to JULIE.

JOHN . . . *wait* . . .

JOHN *holds up a cautious finger to* JULIE. *He looks up and moves to
the stairs, listening for a long moment.*

Finally, he moves back to JULIE *and turns down the radio.*

JOHN I can't do that right now—what you ask—I want to but I don't

dare. Not while we're here, I won't do it again. (*Beat.*) I do *care*
about you . . . don't ever doubt that. You don't, do you, Miss?

JULIE "Miss!" Don't call me that! Just call me "Julie" now—no more
barriers between us. Call me "Julie."

JOHN I can't!! There *are* barriers between us and there always will
be, as long as we stay in this place! There's the past and there's
your father—I've never met someone that I feel so much respect
for! If I see his gloves or his hat on a chair, I suddenly feel small—
if I hear the bell ring I jump like a frightened animal! (*He points.*)
I see his boots there, standing proud and straight and my back
bends . . . I get weak!

JOHN *suddenly moves to the boots and knocks them to the floor.*
Kicking them.

JOHN Superstition, that's all it is! Prejudice and superstition that's
been *drilled* into me since I was child!! (*Kicking at them again.*)
But that can be forgotten. It *can.*

JOHN *goes to* JULIE. *Not holding her but imploring her.*

JOHN Leave with me! Leave with me now! To another place where
people will crawl on their hands and knees when they see the
uniform I wear . . . *their* backs will bend, not *mine*! I wasn't born
to do that . . . to be a servant. To *crawl.* (*Beat.*) I've got character
and guts—just help me reach up as high as one branch! Just *one*!
I may be a servant today but soon I'll be running my own hotel!
In ten years I'll be rich and I can retire . . . I'll travel to Romania
and get myself decorated again . . . and who knows? I may even
end up a *Count* or someone like that!

JULIE . . . how nice for you . . .

JOHN In places like Romania you can still buy a title so I will . . . and I'll make you a Countess! *My* Countess!

JULIE But I don't care about that—I'm leaving this world behind me—John, please tell me you love me; if not, it doesn't matter *what* I am!

JOHN *grows frustrated—he glances up at the wall clock.*

JOHN I'll tell you a thousand times later, but not *here*! We have to keep our heads right now or we'll ruin everything! Make a mess of it! We *have* to look at this like two sensible people . . . (*Sits her down.*) You sit there and I'll go over here . . . (*He sits nearby.*) Now. We'll talk as if nothing's happened. Alright?

JULIE My God! Don't you have any *feelings*?!

JOHN Yes, more than anyone I know! (*Beat.*) But I've also learned to *control* them . . .

JOHN *removes his hand from hers—she stares over at him.*

JULIE You were kissing my *shoe* before, and now you're . . . just . . .

JOHN That was *before*. We have other things to consider now.

JULIE . . . please don't be mean to me . . .

JOHN *gathers himself, working not to get too frustrated or angry. He smiles thinly as he says:*

JOHN I'm not being mean, but we have to be strong here. We made a mistake so let's not repeat it . . . (*Beat.*) Your father is due back at any time so we need to decide on some plans *now*. Do you like my ideas? Do you approve?

JULIE That's . . . it all sounds wonderful to me but let me ask you a question: a thing like that requires a lot of capital . . . do you have it?

JOHN Of course I do! (*Beat.*) I have *expertise*, my professional experience, a knowledge of languages . . . *wines*. That should be more than enough "capital!" Don't you think?

JULIE Yes, but we can't buy train tickets with that . . .

JOHN I *know*! That's why I need a partner. Someone who believes in me and this venture.

JULIE But where can you find someone like that on such short notice?

JOHN *turns to* JULIE *and looks at her: She still doesn't get it.*

JOHN Well, that's up to you . . . if you want to be my partner, that is.

JULIE *Me*? I'm . . . I couldn't possibly do that . . . I hardly have two *dimes* to call my own.

JOHN *nods and stands, moving away from her. Lets out a sigh and then says matter-of-factly:*

JOHN Alright, then. It's off.

JULIE . . . and?

JOHN And nothing. Things stay as they are.

JULIE *What*? (*She stands.*) Do you think that I'm going to stay here, under this roof . . . as your *mistress*? Your *whore*? With everyone pointing their fingers at me . . . laughing behind my back? Do you really think that I can ever face my father again? *Do* you?!

JOHN . . . shhhh . . .

JULIE NO! Take me away from here, away from all this shame and dishonor! Do it now! (*She is waiting for him to speak.*) Oh my God . . . My God! What've *I* done?!

JULIE *bursts into tears.* JOHN *stands and watches her. He glances at* KRISTINE*'s room and turns the radio up a bit.*

JOHN You've done the same thing that every woman before you's done.

JULIE And now you hate me! YOU HATE ME! (*Cries and leans against a wall.*) I'm falling . . . oh God, I'm falling . . .

JOHN If you fall down as far as me I'll pick you back up again.

JULIE *Why* was I even drawn to you? What is the attraction of the weak to the strong? The falling to the rising? Or was it *love*? Is this love—do you even *know* what love is?

JOHN Do *I*? Of course I do! You think I haven't been around *girls* before? That's a laugh!

JULIE Ahhh! I despise everything you say . . . the very words that come out of your mouth!

JOHN Well, that's the way I've learned things and that's who I am!! Don't act so high and mighty, *Miss* . . . you're the same as me now!

JOHN *pulls out a chair for her and motions to it.* JULIE *doesn't move yet.*

JOHN Now come here and don't make such a fuss. I'll pour you a glass of something nice.

JULIE *finally moves to the chair and sits.* JOHN *brings out the bottle of wine from earlier and sets it on the table. He goes to get their used glasses.*

JULIE *picks up the bottle, studies it. Turns to* JOHN.

JULIE Where did you get this?

JOHN The wine cellar.

JULIE It's my *father's* Burgundy!

JOHN Yes. Should be good enough for his future son-in-law.

JULIE . . . and I drank *beer* with you! *I* did!

JOHN Well, that only goes to show your taste is less refined than mine is . . .

JULIE Thief!

JOHN Ha! And who's going to tell on me? *You*?

JULIE Oh my God! I'm the partner of a thief!! How could *this* happen? Am I drunk? Have I been sleepwalking?

JOHN . . . don't play "the innocent" now . . .

JULIE Is there *anyone* more miserable than me?!

JOHN "Miserable?" After your little *conquest*?! Why should *you* be?! (*Points.*) Try thinking of poor Kristine there! Don't you think a *servant's* got any feelings?!

JULIE I did once but now I don't! (*Beat.*) And besides, she's a *cook*. A cook's a cook . . .

JOHN And a whore's a whore.

JULIE*'s eyes go wide. She puts a hand over her mouth.*

JULIE Oh God in Heaven, please end my miserable life—please lift me out of this *wretched* place that I'm in! Please! SAVE ME!!

JOHN I have to admit . . . I almost feel sorry for you. Looking at you there.

JULIE *slumps down in her chair.* JOHN *takes a nearby seat.*

JOHN But when I was a boy . . . there in the onion fields or lying in the muck, watching you on that rose terrace . . . I had the same *bad* thoughts as any child my age.

JULIE But you wanted to *die* for me! You told me that!

JOHN In the *oat bin*? (*Beat.*) No. That was talk, that's all. Just talk.

JULIE A "lie," you mean?

JOHN More or less. I read about it somewhere— a story in a newspaper about a man who crawled into a woodbox filled with elder flowers . . . because he couldn't afford to pay some nagging woman's child support!

JULIE So *this* is the sort of man you are? What you're *really* like?

JOHN Well . . . I had to say *something*.

JULIE YOU BASTARD!

JOHN YOU *BITCH*!

JOHN *makes a show of standing up and tossing his chair aside. Defiant.*

Finally JOHN *rights the chair and sits back down again.*

JULIE Now that you've seen the falcon's back . . .

JOHN Well, I don't know about "back," but . . .

JULIE *I* was your first branch! ME!

JOHN Yes . . . but how could I've known it was all rotten inside?!

JULIE I was going to be the *sign* on your hotel!

JOHN And I'd be the *hotel*! *I* would!

JULIE . . . sit at your little desk, smile at all the customers and pad their bills . . .

JOHN No, I'd do that myself.

JULIE How can someone be *so* filthy?! HOW?!

JOHN Go wash yourself clean if you don't like it!

JULIE *stands up. Stamping her foot as she moves closer.*

JULIE Get up when I speak to you! You *lackey!* You *servant!*
JOHN Servant's *whore!* Poor man's *slut!* (*Stands.*) Shut your mouth
and get away from here!!

JOHN, *on his feet now, squares off with her. Imposing his bulk on
her—*JULIE *takes an involuntary step back.*

JOHN *Who* are you to lecture me?! Have you *ever* seen one of your
own maids go after a man the way that you have tonight?! Ever
seen a girl in my class *begging* for it the way you did?! *I* haven't.
Only in animals and pathetic little *tramps* like you . . .

Suddenly the wind goes out of JULIE*'s sails and she drops her shoulders. Head bowed. Standing there like a broken little girl.*

JULIE (*Beaten.*) . . . that's right. Hurt me. Crush me to the ground.
That's what I deserve. I'm worthless. Rotten. (*Puts her arms out
to him.*) Please help me out of this if there's a way . . . *please*, John!!
JOHN I can't deny my part in seducing you . . .

JULIE *remains with her arms open. Waiting. Instead of going to her, however,* JOHN *continues after her:*

JOHN . . . but do you think that I would've dared to even *look* at
you—someone like *me*, in my position—if you hadn't *invited* me
in? Hmmmm? (*Beat.*) I'm still amazed myself . . .

JULIE . . . and *proud* . . .

JOHN Why not! Although it was probably just a bit too easy to make
it very exciting.

JULIE That's right. Go on. Hit me some more . . .

JULIE *slaps at herself, repeatedly smacking her own face and body. He
watches this for a moment then goes to her.* JOHN *puts his arms around
her to stop it.*

JOHN No, I'm sorry I said that—I never hit a person when they're
down, especially if it's a woman . . . (*Beat.*) I can't say I'm surprised to find out that all your glitter was a trick of the light and
that the falcon's back is just as gray as its belly. (*Wiping her tears.*)
I knew that shine on your cheek was nothing more than powder
and that dirty nails and a filthy handkerchief aren't clean just
because they have perfume splashed on them. I knew all that!
(*Studies her.*) On the other hand, it saddens me to know I wasn't
chasing something greater . . . a better class of person . . .
it hurts me to watch you sink lower than your own cook. Hurts
like watching the autumn flowers beaten down by the rain and
turned into muck . . .

JOHN *releases her and walks away. Goes over and picks up his
employer's boots. Places them back on a chair.*

JULIE You talk as though you're already above me . . .

JOHN I *am*. Fact is I can make you my *Countess* but you'll never turn
me into a *Count*.

JULIE *I* am something you'll never be . . . I come from good *stock*!
I have *blood* in me that you can never touch!! NEVER!!

JOHN   (*Quietly.*) . . . I already have . . .

JOHN *points to the hem of her skirt. It has blood on it.* JULIE *looks down and grows weak. She moves to a seat and sits down.*

She studies her dress and sees blood on the inside of her legs as well.

JOHN *goes to the sink, gets a wet cloth and comes back to her. Kneeling at her feet.*

JOHN   . . . I can even be the *father* of Counts. I've proved that at least, haven't I?

JULIE   You've proved you're a *thief*, that's all.

JOHN *nods at this, dabbing at her dress. He presses open her legs and wipes away the blood from there, too.*

JOHN   There's worse things than being a thief. When I take a job, come into a family . . . I consider myself a part of that family. Like one of its own children. Can someone really deny me plucking a sweet berry off the bush when its fruit is dangling down so close to the ground? Hmmmm?

JOHN *puts the cloth aside and buries his head in her lap.* JULIE *doesn't stop him. She simply waits.*

JOHN   *Julie* . . . you're such a perfect woman . . . too good for the likes of me! You were drunk and tired . . . you let yourself go . . . and now you're trying to cover that up by telling yourself that you love me, but you don't! Yes, you might've been attracted to me . . . but then your love's no better than mine was! That just makes us animals—we could never be happy that way—and I know you'll never *really* love me. I *know* it!

JULIE *How*?! How can you be certain?!

JULIE puts her hands on JOHN's face and turns it up to her own. They stare at each other. Hoping against hope.

JOHN . . . you mean there's a chance? Of course I *could* fall in love with you! A woman like you . . . you're beautiful, refined, lovable when you want to be, cultivated. The fire you start in a man's heart wouldn't burn out any time soon! (*Stands and pulls her close.*) You're like a fine, hot wine—one kiss from you . . . it's enough to . . .

They kiss again. Losing themselves in each other. JOHN pulls back, leading JULIE toward his room once more but she stops him. Tears herself out of his grasp.

JULIE No! NO! Let me go!! You won't get me *that* way again . . . not anytime soon!

JOHN How then?! HOW?! Not by getting on my knees and bowing at your feet! I've already *done* it! Not by caresses and pretty speeches! Not by saving you from disgrace! I'VE TRIED THAT!! SO HOW THEN?!

JULIE I DON'T KNOW! I DON'T KNOW HOW!! I hate you! I *hate* you but I *can't* escape you!!

JOHN Then escape *with* me!!

JULIE "Escape?" (*Thinks.*) Yes, we must escape! But . . . I'm so tired
. . . give me a glass of wine before we go . . .

JOHN *does as she asks—he pours her a glass of wine and she drinks
it down. She holds out her glass for more.*

JULIE We need to talk . . . we still have a little more time . . .

JOHN Don't drink so much. (*Pouring her more.*) You'll get drunk and
we can't have that.

JULIE What difference does it make?

JOHN The *difference* is you look cheap, *that's* what! (*Beat.*) Now,
what were you going to say to me?

JULIE We *have* to get out of here . . . we've *got* to leave . . . but
we need to speak about things first! We must! Or should I say,
I must. You've done all the talking up until now, told me your
story, but you should know my story as well . . . before we leave
this place.

JOHN Wait! Just . . . excuse me a moment . . . but are you sure
about this? You might regret it if you tell me all your secrets. Not
now, but later . . .

JULIE Aren't you my friend? You said you were.

JOHN Yes . . . but you should never count on me.

JULIE You don't mean that. Besides, everybody knows my secrets
already—my mother was not born into this life. She came from
a very humble background . . . she was brought up to believe
things like women's rights, equality of the sexes. All that. Even
the idea of *marriage* repelled her . . . and when my father proposed
to her, she refused . . . said she could never be his wife but that
she would be his lover. Still, she finally consented in the end.
(*Beat.*) And then *I* came into the world . . . against her wishes, so

far as I can tell. I was left to run wild, be a true child of nature, but I also had to learn everything that any boy could learn, so that I was the proof that a woman is just as good as a man. I was even made to dress in boys' clothing . . . (*Beat.*) I learned to tend horses but could never milk cows. I groomed, harnessed and hunted. I was even forced to be witness to the slaughter! It was disgusting! (*Beat.*) The men were given the women's jobs and the women were given the men's jobs until the whole place fell to pieces . . . we were the laughingstock of the county!! You *must've* heard the stories!! (*Beat.*) Father finally came to his senses and began to return the estate back to the way it was. Not long after, my mother became ill. I'm not sure what it was, but it was awful. She had convulsions . . . hid in the attic and the garden . . . sometimes didn't even come home at night . . . (*Beat.*) Then came the big fire, which I know that people still talk about. The stables, the barn and even the house . . . destroyed. Arson was strongly suggested since it happened only a *day* after the insurance had expired. Father's quarterly payment had been delayed by a messenger's carelessness . . . and . . . so . . .

JULIE *stops for a moment, drifting off. She looks at her glass of wine and drinks. Nearly finishes it.*

JOHN You need to stop now . . .

JULIE Why? Who cares? (*Beat.*) . . . anyhow, we were absolutely destitute after that. We were sleeping in the *outbuildings*. Father had no idea where to get the loan to rebuild. Then one day, from nowhere, my mother suggested that he should take money from a childhood friend of hers . . . a local brick manufacturer who

had offered to help. Father borrowed from him but he wasn't
allowed to pay back any interest . . . which surprised him.
(*She has another sip.*) So: the estate was rebuilt. (*Beat.*) Do
you know who started that fire?

JOHN   Your mother.

JULIE   Mmmmm. And do you know who that man was? The brick
manufacturer?

JOHN   Your . . . mother's lover . . .

JULIE   Yes! Right again! (*Beat.*) And do you know whose money it
was? Do you?

JOHN   Wait . . . it must've been . . . no. I don't.

JULIE   It was my mother's.

JOHN   You mean . . . no, your father's, too. Unless they had some
kind of arrangement . . . ?

JULIE   Not an *arrangement*. She just didn't want him having any
control over it—she had a small inheritance of her own—and so
she had entrusted it to her "friend."

JOHN   Who hid it away.

JULIE   Exactly! He kept it for her. My father found out about it . . .
but of course he couldn't bring it to court. He couldn't pay back
her lover, couldn't even prove that it was *her* money! It was her
revenge for him taking control of the estate and forcing her to
marry him. Father tried to take his own life—there were rumors
of a failed attempt to shoot himself—but that didn't happen.
He lived. He also got back at my mother for what she'd done.
He made her *pay* . . . you can't imagine how terrible those five
years were. I loved my father but naturally I sided with my mother.
I didn't know all the facts at that point. I learned from her to hate
men; she hated the whole *lot* of you, the entire sex—you *must've*
heard stories about that!—and so she brought me up to feel the

same. I promised her that I would never become the slave of any man. Not ever.

JOHN I see. (*Beat.*) But you got engaged to that lawyer.

JULIE Yes. To make him *my* slave.

JOHN . . . but he wouldn't follow your lead? Is that it?

JULIE No, not true at all! . . . I just grew tired of him. . . .

JOHN So is that what I saw in the stable yard? You "breaking it off" with him?

JULIE (*Defensively.*) What did you see?

JOHN How "you" broke off the engagement. You can still see it there, on your cheek . . . (*Pointing.*) . . . where he hit you.

JULIE *instinctively touches a spot on her cheek. Flushed.*

JULIE (*Defensively.*) *That's* a lie! *I'm* the one who ended it! Is that what he said, that he . . . ?! (*She stops.*) The *bastard*!!

JOHN "Bastard?" I don't think so, Miss. You just said . . . you hate all men.

JULIE *Yes*! Most of the time . . . except . . . when the burning comes . . . inside me. Then it's like it might never stop . . .

JOHN And *me*? Do you hate me, too?

JULIE More than anyone! I'd like to watch you slaughtered like a beast . . .

JOHN Sure! Kill me like a rabid dog, why not? Or like your *own* dog . . . for that matter. (*Beat.*) You run free and the animal dies. That's the way it works.

JULIE *stares at him—no answer back to what he's said so* JOHN *continues:*

JOHN   Problem being, you haven't got a gun and there's no animal

here . . . it's just you and me. So what do we do now?

JULIE   Run.

JOHN   Run where? And *why* . . . just to make each other's life hell?

JULIE   *No*!! To be happy, just for a moment . . . a day or two . . .

a week . . . for as long as we can . . . until we kill ourselves.

JOHN   "Kill ourselves?!" Why do that? Better we open a hotel . . .

JULIE   (*Drifting.*) . . . yes . . . on the shore of Lake Como . . . the sun

is always shining there . . . and we can have green laurels at

Christmas . . . oranges growing on the trees . . .

JOHN   Lake Como is a *swamp*—a rainy hell—and the only oranges

I ever saw were in the shops! But: it is a lovely spot for tourists.

Lots of little *villas* to be rented out to loving couples. Know why?

Because they all sign leases for six months but they're gone in

three *weeks*!

JULIE   Why so quickly . . . ?

JOHN   Because that's how long it takes for them to drive each other

insane! However, the rent is paid in full and you can rent it out

again to someone else . . . and so on! *Lots* of love in that place,

even if it doesn't last very long.

JULIE *suddenly goes to* JOHN, *pulling him close. Studying him.*

JULIE   . . . don't you want to die with me?

JOHN   I don't want to die at *all*!! First off, I like living! And second,

I think doing that—killing yourself—it's a sin.

JULIE   "A sin?" So you believe in God?

JOHN   Of course I do! And I go to church, too—every other Sunday.

(*Beat.*) Listen, I'm tired of this. I'm going back to bed . . .

JULIE No you're not! You think you can walk out on this so easily?! Hmmm? Walk away from a woman that you've *ruined*?!! You *owe* me something!!

JOHN *stares at her for a moment. He reaches into a pocket and pulls out a silver dollar. Slaps it onto the table.*

JOHN There. Consider my debt fully paid.

JULIE And do you know what the law says about this?

JOHN Unfortunately there's no law for when a woman seduces a man . . .

JULIE Do you really see any other way out of this . . . other than running away, getting married and then divorcing? *Do* you?

JOHN Maybe I don't like that idea so much. We seem like a bad match . . .

JULIE A "bad match?"

JOHN Yes. For *me*. I've got better parentage than you do—there aren't any *arsonists* in my family.

JULIE Are you so sure about that?

JOHN No, but you certainly can't prove otherwise. We don't keep family records; well, except for what the police have . . . (*Beat.*) But I've seen that big book upstairs, in the study—it's filled with all kinds of scandals—and now I know first-hand the story of your own parents. I don't have anything like that in *my* past! I might not have any "great men" in my family but I still might become one myself . . .

JULIE That's what I get for confiding in a man like you . . . for *sacrificing* my honor!

JOHN "Sacrificing!" You fell on that sword pretty easily, seems to me. (*Beat.*) And don't say I didn't warn you. Drinking makes you talk . . . and one should *never* talk too much. At least not about themselves . . .

JULIE Oh God, I regret everything! (*Looking at* JOHN.) If only you *loved* me . . .

JOHN JUST STOP IT! What am I supposed to do?! Hmm? Cry and kiss you and jump over your riding crop? Lure you off to Lake Como for three weeks . . . and then what? WHAT?! (*Beat.*) This is getting painful now but that's what happens when you get mixed up with women. (*Beat.*) Listen, Miss . . . *Julie* . . . I know that you're unhappy, I can see that you're suffering, but I don't understand you. This isn't—my people don't carry on like this . . . we don't *hate* each other! Love is a game, it's for *fun* when we finally get time off from work but we don't have all day and night to do it like you do! (*Going to her.*) I think you're sick, Miss. I think your family has poisoned you and your well-being is in danger . . .

JULIE Then be *kind* to me! (*Softer.*) At least now you're talking to me like a human being.

JOHN So then act like a human being yourself! You *spit* on me and then you're surprised when I *wipe* it back on you . . .

JULIE (*Pleadingly.*) John, help me!! PLEASE HELP ME!! Tell me what to do . . . where to go . . .

JOHN Christ, as if I know!

JULIE . . . I was insane . . . driven by lust . . . but . . . there must be some way out . . .

JOHN *glances over at* KRISTINE*'s room—he looks back at* JULIE *quickly, covering as he says:*

JOHN   Yes, if we stay exactly where we are and we try to be calm.
Nobody knows anything.

JULIE   That's impossible! People will find out! (*Pointing at* KRISTINE*'s
room.*) Kristine knows!

JOHN   She doesn't know for sure. (*Beat.*) Anyway, nobody'll ever
believe her . . .

JULIE *mulls this over quickly—accepts it for the moment. She turns
back to* JOHN. *Their eyes meet.*

JULIE   But . . . it could happen again.

JOHN   It could.

JULIE   And then what? (*Beat.*) Or . . . what if it already doesn't
matter?

JOHN   What do you mean?

JULIE   The *consequences* . . .

JOHN *suddenly stops—now here's a thought his quicksilver mind
hasn't had yet. The color drains from his face.* JOHN *looks at* JULIE,
a little panic rising in his voice.

JOHN   . . . why didn't *I* think of that? You're right. (*Beat.*) You have
to go. *Now.* By the time your father gets back. (*Goes to her.*) You
need to leave! Alone! Not with me, that would give us away. You
have to go. Go upstate . . . go abroad . . . just go somewhere!
Anywhere! NOW!

JULIE   *Alone?* Where? I can't do that!

JOHN   You *have* to, and before your father gets here!! If you don't,
we both know what's going to happen! (*Beat.*) Once you've made
a mistake, you just keep making it, figuring the deed is done so

"why not?" You just get more and more careless until it's too late. Until you get caught.

JOHN *goes to* JULIE *and holds her by the shoulders. Not rough but speaking seriously to her:*

JOHN That's why you've got to go away. Now. Later you can write to your father and confess everything to him—except that it was *me*! He'd never guess that, and I don't think he'll be too keen on figuring out the truth.

JULIE I'll go if you'll come with me . . .

JOHN *releases her, frustrated by the impossibility of her statement. Her way of thinking.*

JOHN Have you honestly gone crazy?! I mean . . . "Heiress Runs Off With Valet!" I can see it now, it'll be in every paper up and down the coast in three days and a month from now, your father'll be in ruins . . . he'll never survive it!

JULIE (*Tearful.*) I can't go and I can't stay! HELP ME! I'm so tired . . . I can't—order me! *Make* me go!

JOHN Now do you see?!! Huh?!! Do you *see* just how miserable you people are?! *Strutting* around here with your *noses* in the air . . . as if you were God's *gift* to creation, as if you *owned* the world! *One* thing happens and you all fall to pieces!! (*Beat.*) Fine! You want orders? I'll give you orders! Go upstairs, get dressed and hurry up!! Find some money for travel—I don't care where or how, just do it—and come back down as fast as you can! (*In her face.*) DO IT NOW!

JULIE (*Pleading.*) . . . come upstairs with me . . . *John* . . .

JOHN   TO *YOUR* ROOM?! (*Laughs.*) You're actually crazy! *Insane!*
Now go! GO RIGHT NOW!!

JULIE *remains in the room, unsure what to do. She seems stunned.*
Shell-shocked.

JOHN *goes to her, pushing her along. Toward the stairs.* JULIE *is*
hesitant but JOHN *uses his size to keep moving her out the door.*

JOHN   GO! *GO!!* GET OUT OF HERE!!

JULIE   . . . please don't be cruel to me . . .

JOHN   *Orders* always sound cruel! Maybe now you'll know what it
feels like . . .

JOHN *gives her another little shove and* JULIE *bursts into tears. She*
stands there, helpless, weeping. JOHN *looks at the clock on the wall.*
Finally, he goes to her and gives her a hug. A kiss on the cheek. Tries
again to move her.

JULIE *tries to gather herself—manages to stop crying and to begin*
sniffling—and to make her way up and outside.

JOHN *comes back down the stairs, unsure what to do next. He goes*
to a drawer and gets out a little note pad and a pencil. He goes to the
radio and turns it off.

JOHN *sits at the table. Starts to make calculations on a piece of paper.*
Adds numbers together quickly in his head (and sometimes aloud).

KRISTINE *appears from her room. Dressed for church. She carries*
a shirt and tie in one hand. A purse in the other.

She moves to JOHN *and places a hand on his shoulder. He jumps and rises up. Realizes it's* KRISTINE *and sighs a breath of relief.*

JOHN *hugs* KRISTINE *and then pulls away from her. She is just staring at him. Uncomfortable, he is about to sit down again but thinks better of it.*

Instead he goes over to put away the glasses and bottles on the counter. His back to KRISTINE.

KRISTINE . . . what've you been up to?

JOHN (*Turning.*) Nothing. Just . . . I was keeping Miss Julie company. That's all.

KRISTINE "Miss *Julie*?"

JOHN You know who I mean! (*Beat.*) She was . . . didn't you hear us talking?

KRISTINE *doesn't speak for a moment. Just looks at* JOHN *instead. Finally:*

KRISTINE I slept like a log.

JOHN *nods at this and continues to clean up.* KRISTINE *is watching him.*

JOHN I see. (*Beat.*) And so you're dressed for church already . . .

KRISTINE Yes . . . and you promised me you'd come for Communion this time. Remember?

JOHN That's right. I remember. (*Thinks.*) Fine. Help me with those . . .

JOHN *points to the shirt and tie.* KRISTINE *nods. She gets the tie prepared and unbuttons the shirt while* JOHN *pulls down his braces and buttons up his trousers.*

JOHN . . . what's the lesson for today?

KRISTINE The beheading of John the Baptist.

JOHN *throws her a look as he slips into the open shirt.* KRISTINE *does her best "Mona Lisa" while she winds the tie around his neck. Pulls it tightly in both hands.*

JOHN God! That'll take an eternity! (*She pulls firmly on the knot.*) Hey! Stop!! That's too tight, you're choking me!!

KRISTINE *doesn't let go—she slaps away his hand and then continues to help* JOHN *dress. He yawns while she works.*

JOHN . . . I'm so tired . . .

KRISTINE That's what you get for staying up late! (*Beat.*) Why was she here *so* long?

JOHN I told you already! (*Points upstairs.*) She wouldn't stop *talking* . . . I mean . . .

KRISTINE That girl will never learn how to behave!

JOHN I know.

The conversation stops as KRISTINE *keeps looking over at* JOHN. *He busies himself—tucks his shirt in carefully and pulls up his braces. He finds a comb and runs it through his hair. Cleans his shoes with a rag. Checks the time.*

JOHN You know, Kristine . . . it's strange . . .

KRISTINE What is?

JOHN Nothing. I just . . . mean about her.

KRISTINE What's so strange about *her*? Hmmm?

JOHN Everything. It's all . . . just . . . (*Beat.*) Listen . . . there's something I want to say to you . . .

KRISTINE *has been tidying up a few things on the counter.* JOHN *watches her every move. She turns, pointing to the empty bottles.*

KRISTINE Were you *drinking* with her? (*Beat.*) Did you drink *beer* with that girl? Tell me.

JOHN . . .

KRISTINE Look me in the eye. (*Beat.*) *Did* you?

JOHN Yes. I was . . . I mean . . . *we* . . .

KRISTINE *is done playing games.* JOHN *knows that she knows the truth and he can't face her. He puts his head down.*

KRISTINE Is it possible? Is this *even* possible?

JOHN Yes, it is. I'm sorry.

KRISTINE Uhhhhh! I never would've believed it . . . (*Beat.*) The *shame* of it!

JOHN Listen, you're not jealous of *her*, are you? Because . . . it's . . .

KRISTINE No! Not her—if it'd been *Clara* or someone like that, I would've scratched her eyes out—but it still disgusts me!

JOHN So . . . are you angry with her, then?

KRISTINE No. Not her. *You*! That was very cruel of you, it was wrong. Poor thing! (*Beat.*) But I won't stay here now, not in this house.

JOHN . . . *Kristine* . . .

KRISTINE I won't, and I don't care who knows why! I can't work in a house where I've got no respect for the people in it . . .

JOHN Why do you have to *respect* 'em? Why would you *want* to?

KRISTINE You're so clever, why don't you tell me. Do you really want to serve people who can't act decently? Hmm? Do you? If you ask me, you'd only be disgracing yourself . . .

JOHN But . . . at least there'd be the comfort of knowing that they aren't any better than you are . . .

KRISTINE No, I don't think so—if they're the same as us then what's the point? What's there to strive for? (*Beat.*) And just think of her father! He has already had *so* much misery in his life! (*Beat.*) No, I'm not staying in this place another night!!! (*Looks at him.*) And with *you*!! She had to do that with the likes of you . . . not even a lawyer or someone like that . . . a *gentleman* at least . . .

JOHN What's *that* supposed to mean?

KRISTINE Oh, I know, I know . . . you're alright in your way, but there's still a difference between people and "people." (*Thinking.*) No, I'll *never* be able to forget this. A woman like her, the way she acts around men—so *full* of herself—you'd never guess that she'd go and fall into the arms of one . . . especially one like you! (*Laughs.*) And she wanted to have Diana *shot* for running around with the groundskeeper's mutt!! (*Beat.*) That's just . . . no, I'm not staying here any longer. I quit!

JOHN And then what?

KRISTINE Well . . . since you ask . . . you'd better start looking around for something else, too . . . as we've already made plans to marry.

JOHN That's . . . I mean, *look* for what? I could never find another position like this!! Not as a married man . . .

KRISTINE I *know* that! Maybe you could get a job in a hotel, a porter or something like that to start—you talk a good game about the "hotel" business—so why not start there? Or maybe a government job . . . a *clerk*. The pay wouldn't be much but that'll have a bene-fit package and a pension, too . . . for a widow and her children.

JOHN That might be fine for someone else, but it's not my way to start thinking about that . . . a *pension*! A widow and children!! Not at my age . . . I've got bigger plans than that!

KRISTINE Your "plans!" You better stop thinking so much about your plans and start thinking about your "obligations!" You *hear* me?!

JOHN Stop harping about that! Yes, I hear you! My *obligations*, I know! I KNOW! (*Softer.*) I know what I have to do . . . but just . . . there's plenty of time to figure all that out. A few months yet. Right?

JOHN *goes to her and puts his arms around her. Tries his best to soothe her.* KRISTINE *finally calms down.*

JOHN . . . just go finish getting yourself ready for church and I'll . . . we can go soon. I promise.

She buries her face in his shoulder and he holds her for a moment longer. He has no choice.

Sounds from upstairs. Movement. Both of them look up and listen. Surprised and unsure what this means.

KRISTINE Who's wandering around up there so early?

JOHN I don't know . . . maybe it's Clara?

KRISTINE Hmmmmm. (*Listens.*) Surely . . . *he* can't be back without us knowing about it . . . can he? I mean . . . I suppose it's . . .

JOHN (*Nervously.*) No! That's *not* possible! I mean, I think we would've heard, or . . . he would've rung for me . . . right? I mean . . . (*Listening.*) It *couldn't* be him. *No.*

KRISTINE . . . well, whoever it is, I've never seen anything like this . . .

KRISTINE *looks at* JOHN *again and then goes off and out to her room.*

JOHN *stands in the kitchen alone, uncertain as to what to do next. He seems a bit helpless. Like a young boy.*

The sun is starting to shine in through the door upstairs and the room is slowly brightening.

JOHN *sees that* KRISTINE *has left her purse on the table. He goes to it, looking around, then begins to go through it. Searching. He removes some money and pockets it.*

When he turns around he sees JULIE *on the stairs. She is back and watching him. She is dressed for travel and she carries a covered birdcage, a small suitcase and a purse.*

JOHN *motions for her to enter. He closes* KRISTINE*'s purse as she walks down the stairs and moves to the table.*

JULIE . . . I'm ready.

JOHN Shhhhh! Kristine's awake now.

JULIE Does she suspect anything?

JOHN No . . . she's . . . (*Studies* JULIE.) God! *Look* at yourself!

JULIE What's wrong?

JOHN You're pale like a ghost . . . and I'm sorry to say something, but your face . . . there. (*Pointing.*) It's dirty.

JULIE Oh . . . well, then I'll wash it . . .

JULIE *sets down her luggage and the birdcage. She goes to a basin and begins to wash her face and hands.*

JULIE Could you get me a towel, please? (*She looks up the stairs.*) Look . . . the sun is rising. So beautiful.

JOHN . . . yes . . . and with it all the demons will go away. They'll disappear.

JULIE Well, we were both *possessed* last night, that's for certain . . . (*Beat.*) John, come with me now. *Please* come. (*Points to her purse.*) I have money.

JOHN Yes, but enough?

JULIE Enough for now. For the two of us. (*She speaks earnestly.*) I can't travel alone, not today. A holiday. A stuffy train . . . packed with crowds and all of them just *staring* at me . . . dozens of stops . . . and I *have* to get away! I can't, though . . . I'm not able to without you! And memories . . . the memories will come flooding back to me, of this place and being at church . . . the tables covered in oak leaves and lilacs . . . dinners with family and friends and afternoons on the grounds, laughing and dancing and, and . . . music and flowers and games! (*Starts to cry.*) No matter how far or fast I flee . . . those memories will follow after me in the baggage car! The *shame* . . . and *guilt* . . .

JULIE *is a mess. Emotional and on the verge—*JOHN *sees now that he has to do something drastic. He glances at* KRISTINE*'s room and then turns to* JULIE. *Nods his head.*

JOHN ALRIGHT! Yes, I'll go with you! I'll do it but we have to go now! Do you hear me? *NOW*. THIS MINUTE. Before it's too late . . .

JULIE *moves quickly and throws her arms around* JOHN. *She pulls him close, hugging him and shutting her eyes. After a moment she lets him go and says:*

JULIE Get dressed then!

JOHN But no bags! It'll just give us away.

JULIE No, nothing. Only what we can carry on.

JOHN *nods and goes off—pulls on his jacket and returns. He stops and looks at the covered cage. Turning to* JULIE *and pointing.*

JOHN What've you got there?

JULIE It's only a finch. I can't possibly leave her behind . . .

JOHN What, carry a *birdcage* along with us? To *bang* against everything and for everyone to *gawk* at?! You must've lost your mind! LEAVE IT RIGHT WHERE IT IS.

JULIE *goes to it and puts a protective arm around it—pleading with* JOHN *as she tries to block him from it.*

JULIE It's the only thing from this house that I've brought with me . . . the only living thing that cares for me, now that Diana has deserted me! Don't be cruel! Let me take her . . .

JOHN Shhhh! Leave it there, I said, and don't speak so loud. Kristine will hear you . . .

JULIE That's not . . . *no*! I won't just leave her with anyone! I *won't*! I'd rather kill her first!

JOHN *You*! You mean me, right?! *Me*!! So just say it, then! SAY IT!

JULIE Yes, you! YOU! (*Desperate.*) Please . . .

JOHN FINE!

JOHN *crosses quickly to the counter and grabs up a knife. Motions for* JULIE *to grab the cage.*

JOHN Bring it here and I'll cut its head off.

JULIE Alright . . . but don't *hurt* her . . . (*Stopping.*) No, I can't! I *can't*!

JOHN Yes, you can . . . *I* can! *I'll* do it!

JULIE *can tell that* JOHN *means business—she removes the little bird from the cage and holds it carefully. Moving slowly toward* JOHN *and his knife.*

JULIE . . . poor little bird . . . Why do you have to die? Do you die for *me*?

JOHN God, don't make such a scene! Your whole *life* is at stake! Hurry up!!

She approaches JOHN *and he snatches the bird out of her hand. He holds it down and raises the knife.* JULIE *backs away.*

JOHN They should've forced you to *kill* a few things instead of just making you *watch*. (*Chops off the bird's head.*) You wouldn't be so faint at the sight of blood . . .

JOHN *tosses the carcass and the knife aside. Goes to wipe his hands clean when* JULIE *explodes. Runs at him, starts to beat on his back with her fists.*

JOHN *turns to defend himself but she keeps clawing at him while she screams:*

JULIE AHHHHHH! KILL ME!! KILL ME TOO!!!

JOHN *gets his arms around her but she continues to shout and thrash about.*

JULIE You can slaughter an innocent thing without even batting a lash!! I HATE YOU!! I DESPISE YOU!!! Now there's blood between us and I curse the moment I ever laid my eyes on you!! I curse the moment I first had life in my mother's womb!!

JOHN STOP IT! What good does any of this do?! This "cursing" of yours?! WE HAVE TO GO!

JULIE No! No, I'm not ready to go yet!! *NO!!*

JOHN *continues to struggle with* JULIE. *She finally gets free of his hold and pulls away. Turns toward the stairs when they both stop and listen.*

JULIE . . . what's that? Was that the sound of an *automobile* approaching?

JOHN *takes an involuntary step back, looking around. His body coiled and tense.*

JULIE *listens but then turns her attentions back to this man in front of her. She is venomous now and spews it all out at* JOHN:

JULIE You think I'm afraid of a little blood?! You think I'm *so* weak?! Hmmm? (*Beat.*) I'd like to see *your* blood . . . see your brains and your sex *swimming* in blood there on the chopping block!!! Every last one of you!!! I would *drink* out of your skull . . . I'd *bathe* my feet in the hole torn into your chest and roast your heart over an open flame and eat it whole! DO YOU HEAR ME?! You think I'm weak because I let you love me? Because I *ached* to be touched and to have your seed in me? You think I want to carry your child under my heart, feed it with my soul?!! Give it your *name*?!! (*Beat.*) I don't even *know* your name! Your *family* name . . . do you even have one?! I'm not so sure! "Mr. Servant," maybe, or . . . "Mr. Shithouse," that might be it! Yes!! That sounds about right!!

JOHN *stands and takes this abuse. He doesn't drop his gaze—he stares straight at* JULIE *as she hurls insult after insult at him. Hissing with invectives.*

JULIE   You *dog* wearing *my* collar!! You *mongrel* eating scraps off *my* table! I share you with a cook! I'm my own servant's rival! (*Calming down.*) You think I'm the coward who'll run away? Hmmm? No . . . just watch. I'm staying now, no matter what happens! Father will be home soon! He'll find his desk broken into—his money gone—and he will ring that bell twice! Ring for his valet! (*Points.*) And when he doesn't come he'll phone up the police, and I'll tell him everything. EVERYTHING! What a relief that'll be, to finally have an end to it, all of this . . . *if* that is the end!! Maybe he'll have a stroke and die and that'll be the end of *all* of us! Everyone here. For a moment there'll be peace and calm. Quiet. But not for you . . . you'll be gone. Taken away and gone! (*Snaps her fingers.*) Just like that. And your little one will end up in some orphanage . . . the *bastard* . . . son of a valet who ends up in jail; just like the man who came before him.

JULIE *is finished and grows silent. Starting at him.* JOHN *slowly claps his hands at her. Doing his best to call her bluff.*

JOHN   (*Evenly.*) . . . bravo, Miss. Bravo. Spoken like a true *aristocrat*.

Stalemate to a classic struggle: a "man" and a "woman" facing off and neither one giving way.

KRISTINE *enters and immediately stops. She takes in the entire scene instantly: the dead bird and the cage, the mistress of the house downstairs again and dressed for traveling,* JOHN *poised and acting familiar with her.*

Instead of reacting, however, she is forced to respond to JULIE *(who runs to her and throws herself into* KRISTINE*'s arms).*

JULIE Help me, Kristine! Help me against this man!!

KRISTINE *pries* JULIE *off of herself but keeps the young woman behind her. Protected and away from* JOHN.

KRISTINE What a way to behave! *Both* of you! And on a *Sunday*!! (*Looking again at the bird and the bloody counter.*) What's all this mess? All this shouting and carrying on?!

JULIE You're a woman, Kristine, and you're my friend! Watch out for this man! *Beware!* He's evil!!

KRISTINE *doesn't say anything in return, she just turns and looks at* JOHN. *He shrugs, unsure how to play it now. Finally, he yawns and turns toward his room. Pointing.*

JOHN (*Matter-of-factly.*) Say what you want about me . . . I'll leave you ladies to it. I'm going for a shave.

He removes his jacket and hangs it on a hook just out of sight. He exits.

KRISTINE *begins to lead* JULIE *over to the table and into a seat.* JULIE *continues to speak rapidly throughout:*

JULIE . . . you've got to listen to me, Kristine!! You *have* to understand!!

KRISTINE No, I don't "have" to because I *don't*!! I don't understand any of this!! Why're you dressed for traveling and why did he have his jacket on? Hmmmmm? (*Beat.*) *Why*, Miss?

JULIE Listen to me, Kristine, and I'll explain; I'll tell you everything!

KRISTINE I don't *want* to know everything!

JULIE Please! You *must*! You must listen to me!

KRISTINE Listen to what? What you've been up to with John? I don't care about that! I couldn't care less . . . it's none of my business, Miss!

KRISTINE *bursts into tears. She wipes them away savagely with the back of her hand.* JULIE *goes to embrace her but to no avail—*KRISTINE *pulls away and puts her hand out to stop* JULIE *from trying again.*

KRISTINE But: if you try to *trick* or lure him into going away with you, *skipping* out on his life here . . . then I *will* put up a fuss! Count on that! I'll put a stop to what you're doing here this minute . . .

JULIE Kristine, listen to me!! We can't stay here—I can't and neither can John! We *have* to go! Please try to understand . . .

KRISTINE . . . why should I?

JULIE *looks off, hoping that* JOHN *will return but he does not.* KRISTINE *is staring holes through* JULIE *and suddenly a thought clicks in* JULIE*'s mind. She blurts out:*

JULIE Wait . . . I've got an idea. No, just hear me out. (*Beat.*) What if
we all went away—the three of us, together—to Europe and then
to wherever we wanted? We could all . . . we could open a *hotel*
. . . and . . . and then . . .

KRISTINE   . . . I've heard this one before . . .

JULIE No, but I have money! Here! *Look*!! (*Goes to her purse and
opens it.*) See? John and I could manage the whole thing . . .
and you could . . . I'm imagining that you'd be best in the kitchen.
Right? *Managing* the kitchen. Yes? (*Beat.*) Say "yes," Kristine, say
that you'll do it! That would make *everything* settled! Please do!
Say "yes!!"

JULIE *is getting worked up now—she's a volatile mix of exhausted,
scared, excited. She is near tears.* KRISTINE *continues to just watch
and listen.*

JULIE *tries to emphasize her point by pulling out handful after handful
of bank notes. Scattering them carelessly across the table and down
onto the floor. Everywhere.*

KRISTINE   . . .

JULIE You've never traveled before, have you, Kristine? You could
get out and see the world!! You can't imagine how wonderful it'd
be going by train . . . new faces, new countries, all the time . . .
we could stop in Germany . . . *Hamburg* . . . and see the zoo!
You'd like that! We'll go to the theater and to the opera . . . and
then on to Munich where they have such beautiful museums!
Filled with Rubens and Raphael, all the great painters. You've
heard of *Munich*, haven't you? I *know* you have! It's where King
Ludwig lived . . . that king who went insane . . . we could see his

castles! All of them are still there, like in some fairy tale! And from there . . . why, it's only a short distance into the Alps and then on to Switzerland. (*Beat.*) Did you know they've got snow on them, even in the summer? The Alps do! And there'd be oranges . . . and . . . and . . . laurels that're green all the year round . . .

JULIE *stops, pausing for breath and to see how any of this has landed with* KRISTINE. *She turns and notices that* JOHN *is standing in his doorway. Freshly shaved. Still holding his razor.*

JULIE   . . . and we can open a hotel there! (*To* JOHN.) Tell her we can! Tell her it's true!! (*Back to* KRISTINE.) I'll sit at the desk when John receives the guests or goes out shopping or writes letters and you'll . . . you'll be . . . oh, Kristine, *that's* the life, I promise you! Train whistles blowing and people arriving, bells ringing up in the rooms and down in the restaurant . . . and you'll be the *lady* of the kitchen! Of course . . . you won't be standing over the stove, no, because you'll have to dress nicely and neatly since people will be seeing you. (*Smiling.*) With your looks—and I'm not just flattering you—I'm sure in no time you'll meet someone and be married yourself . . . a rich Englishman or that type . . . they're easy to find over there . . . and then we'll all get rich! (*Tiring out now.*) We'll . . . we'll build a villa on Lake Como and . . . and we'll . . . I mean, of *course* it can rain there sometimes . . . of course it can!! But the sun shines, too . . . it *has* to shine occasionally! It *has* to!! And that's when we'll . . . even if it grows dark . . . we can go home and be . . . we'll just . . . sometimes . . .

JULIE *is simply babbling now, unsure what else to say or who to say it to. She sits down in a heap. Spent.*

JOHN *doesn't say a word. He glances up at the clock and then moves over to the table. Takes a look at all that cash.* KRISTINE *watches him, then turns to* JULIE. *Says:*

KRISTINE . . . listen to yourself. Do you actually believe any of that, Miss?

JULIE . . . do I *believe* it?

KRISTINE Yes!

JULIE I'm . . . I don't know what I believe . . . I'm not sure I believe in anything any more . . .

Utterly beside herself, JULIE *puts her head down on her arm. Resting on the table.*

JOHN *sets his razor down on the table as he is about to reach out and touch some of that money. He even manages to get a bill or two between his fingers before* KRISTINE *stops him with her voice:*

KRISTINE So . . . you're hoping to escape now, are you?

JOHN I wouldn't exactly call it *escaping*; let's not exaggerate here. You heard her plan . . . even if she is tired . . .

KRISTINE . . . and half out of her mind . . .

JOHN *And* "half out of her mind!" Fine! (*Beat.*) It's still not impossible . . .

KRISTINE Listen to you! (*Scoffs.*) As if I'd cook for the likes of you two! You and your little . . . "Miss *Julie*" . . .

KRISTINE *crosses herself at this while* JOHN *jumps to his feet.*
JULIE *doesn't even flinch at this. She is lost and in a daze.*

JOHN Here now, you just watch what you say! Understand? She's still your *mistress* . . .

KRISTINE "Mistress!"

JOHN Yes! That's right!

KRISTINE Ha! That's a fine name for what she is!

JOHN If you despise her for what she's done, then go ahead and despise yourself for the same *damn* reason!! (*Beat.*) Just you remember that . . . and maybe *next* time do a little more *listening* and a bit less *talking*.

KRISTINE (*Hurt.*) . . . I have a high enough opinion of my own self, thank you . . . I don't need you.

JOHN Yes . . . high enough to look down on others.

KRISTINE At least I don't lower myself . . . I haven't done anything that's beneath me! (*Waits.*) Can't say I've been up to no good with just anyone . . .

JOHN No, you've been lucky enough to have a gentleman like me around . . .

KRISTINE A "gentleman" who'd sell *oats* right out of his employer's barn if he thought he could get away with it!

JOHN *You* should talk! A woman who takes bribes from the butcher!! Commissions from the grocers!! YOU'RE THE SAME AS *ME*, WOMAN! *EXACTLY* THE SAME AS I AM!!

KRISTINE *WHAT*?

JOHN I KNOW WHAT YOU *DO*! (*Laughs.*) And yet you can't stay here "another night" because you can't possibly respect these people! Your *employers*! *You*! DON'T-MAKE-ME-LAUGH!

JOHN *has beaten back* KRISTINE*'s storm, at least for now. She re-groups, adjusts her clothing. Pointing at him.*

KRISTINE Are you coming to church with me? Hmmm? (*Indicating* JULIE.) You could do with a good sermon . . . after the mess you've made!

JOHN No, I'm *not* going to church today! GO BY YOURSELF AND CONFESS YOUR *OWN* SINS!!

KRISTINE *has nothing to say in return. A tear in one eye. Silence between them now.* JULIE *still out of it. Sunlight starting to pour in through the upper archway.*

KRISTINE Yes, I'll do that . . . I'll go and I'll try to bring back enough forgiveness for the both of us . . . our Savior died for all our sins and if you come to Him with an open heart and enough faith . . . penitent . . . then He'll take those sins up onto the cross with Him. (*Crosses herself.*) It's true . . .

JOHN Does that go for *stealing*, too?

KRISTINE *doesn't dignify* JOHN's *response; instead, she goes toward the stairs to leave.*

JULIE—*who has only slightly responded when* KRISTINE *spoke of "forgiveness"—lifts her head a bit more and stops* KRISTINE *with a question:*

JULIE   . . . do you really believe that can happen, Kristine? Like you say?

KRISTINE It's my living faith, Miss, as sure as I am standing here, and I've had it since I was a child . . . it's faith I learned and a belief I've had ever since . . . "Where sin aboundeth . . . there grace aboundeth also!"

JULIE   . . . if only I had your faith . . . if only . . .

KRISTINE   Well, you can't get it by being *rich* . . . it's God's special
grace and He doesn't give it to just anybody.

JULIE   Who does get it, then?

KRISTINE   That's the great secret of grace, Miss . . . He's no
respecter of persons and who they are. With Him the *last* shall
be first . . .

JULIE   . . . then He *does* respect the last . . .

KRISTINE   . . . yes . . . and it's easier for a camel to pass through the
eye of a needle than it is for a rich man to enter the Kingdom of
Heaven. That's just the way it is, Miss.

JULIE *nods and doesn't respond.* KRISTINE *moves toward the steps.*
Passes JOHN *as she goes. Stops and speaks pointedly to him:*

KRISTINE   . . . and I'm telling the chauffeur not to let any cars out
of here while I'm gone, don't think I won't! (*Beat.*) In case you had
an idea about running off and starting a *hotel* or something . . .

KRISTINE *steps away, turns back to say something else but stops her-*
self near the counter. KRISTINE *swallows a sob and suddenly smashes*
the dishes and glasses to the floor. She turns and exits. Up the stairs
and out. Into a shaft of growing sunlight.

JOHN   . . . *bitch.*

JOHN *crosses and sits with* JULIE. *Puts a hand on her back which she*
allows (without gaining any comfort from it).

JOHN   All this because of a little bird . . .

JULIE Forget that now. (*Turning to him.*) Do you see any way out of this? Any way for us to end it properly?

JOHN (*Flatly.*) No. (*Beat.*) We could try and . . . but no. Not really.

JULIE And what would you do if you were me?

JOHN Let's see: A person of *society* . . . a fallen *woman* . . . I don't know. I guess I'd . . . well, maybe I do know . . .

JOHN *'s hand reaches out for the razor.* JULIE *follows his action with her eyes. He pushes the lethal instrument a bit nearer to her. Through the piles of errant money.*

JULIE I see. (*Picking it up and pretending to run it across her throat.*) Like this?

JOHN Yes . . . but *I'd* never do it! I'm . . . that's the difference between us . . . you and me.

JULIE You mean because you're a man and I'm a woman? What does *that* matter?

JOHN Nothing, we're just different. Men and women.

JULIE I want to . . . (*Opening the razor.*) . . . but I can't. I *can't*! (*Beat.*) My father couldn't either . . . when he should've done it.

JOHN No . . . he was right not to! He had to get his revenge first!

JULIE And now my mother'll have revenge again, won't she? Through me . . .

JOHN I dunno. (*Beat.*) Did you ever love your father, Miss?

JULIE Oh yes, tremendously! *Yes*! But I must've hated him, too . . . hated him without even realizing it. My mother as well . . .

JOHN *checks the clock on the wall.* JULIE *watches him and realizes it's almost morning. She continues:*

JULIE They're the ones who brought me up to be half a man and
half a woman . . . so who should I blame? Him? Her? Myself?
I've never even had a "self" to call my own. (*Beat.*) Every thought
I've ever had has come from my father, every emotion from
my mother—I have nothing that's merely mine. *Nothing.* So
who's to blame? Hmmmm? Should I blame Jesus . . . the way
Kristine does? No. I'm too proud for that and far too sensible . . .
thanks to my father. And as for someone rich getting into Heaven,
I think that's a lie! And if it isn't, I still know it won't be Kristine
getting in, what with all the pennies she has tucked away . . .
so who's to blame, John? *Who?* And what's it matter, anyway?
I'm the one who has to carry the guilt . . . who'll face the *gallows*
now . . .

JULIE *smiles at* JOHN, *suddenly resigned to the situation.* JOHN *takes
her hands in his. Trying to be gentle.*

JOHN Yes, but I'm . . . I'm . . . *Julie*, listen . . .

Suddenly there are two sharp rings from one of the bells on the wall.
JULIE *jumps to her feet and so does* JOHN.

JOHN He's back! Your father's *back*! (*Beat.*) My God! God . . . what
if Kristine . . . ?!

They stare at each other for a moment. Another burst of bells. JOHN
*quickly goes and straightens himself up. He pulls on the jacket to
his uniform. He is no longer the man we've seen lounging about—
he is a nervous servant.*

The bells cry out again. Harsh and unforgiving. JULIE *puts a hand over her mouth. Turning white from fear.*

JOHN *crosses slowly to a spot on one wall. He picks up a speaking tube. Presses a button and listens.*

JULIE . . . he might've already been to his desk! John! What if he's . . . ?!

JOHN *furiously waves her off with his free hand, which silences her for a moment. He listens with the tube up to one ear.*

JOHN (*Respectfully.*) Yes, sir? Yes, hello . . . what's that? Yes, sir! Right away, sir! In half an hour . . . Absolutely. (*Beat.*) Thank you, I hope *you* had a nice time as well . . . yes sir. Thank you again. Yes. Good-bye, sir.

JOHN *hangs up and stands there, looking this way and that as his mind races.* JULIE *goes to him. Shakes his arm with both hands.*

JULIE What'd he say? John! *What* did he say?!
JOHN (*Cautiously.*) He's . . . he wants his boots and some coffee in half an hour . . .
JULIE Then there's half an hour . . . before . . .
JOHN . . . we've still got time . . .
JULIE . . . but I'm so tired! I'm just so—I can't think and I can't run and I can't live or even die . . . I CAN'T! I JUST CAN'T!! (*Beat.*) Help me. *Please.* Order me and I'll . . . I'll obey you like a *dog.* I promise I will . . .

JULIE *gets down on her knees, wrapping her arms around the legs of* JOHN. *He stares down at her.*

JULIE   Please, John. *Save* me. Save my honor. That's all I've got left now . . . Do me this last service and save me and my father's good name . . . (*Beat.*) You know what I should do but you can't do it so order *me* . . . make *me* do it and I'll obey.

JOHN   . . . I can't . . .

JULIE   John . . . I'm *begging* you . . .

JOHN   I CAN'T!! It's this damn coat . . . now that I've put it back on, it's like I'm . . . it's the "servant" in me! As soon as that bell rang and I heard his voice again. (*Pulls her to her feet.*) Do you know what? If he came down here right now and asked me to cut my own throat—without even an order, I'm saying, just *asked* me— I bet you I'd do it. I would! Right here on the spot!!

JULIE   Then pretend you're him and I'm you! You gave such a good showing of it earlier, down there on your knees . . . like a real man of the world . . .

JOHN *thinks about this—goes to the table but instead of picking up the razor he starts stuffing the money back into her purse.*

JULIE *goes to him and turns him around. Pleads with him.*

JULIE   . . . or what about one of those hypnotists, like the kind you see at the fair? You've seen them before, surely! (*Beat.*) He asks someone to "Take this broom!" And then a person does just that. They'll pretend to pick it up and . . . and then he'll say "Now sweep! Sweep!" And they do. They sweep . . .

JOHN   . . . but that person's got to be asleep . . .

JULIE . . . I'm already asleep. I feel like I've been sleeping for years . . . and the whole room is filled with smoke . . . your eyes . . . your eyes are glowing like coals in a fire and your face is a patch of light. (*Puts her hands on his face.*) It's nice and warm and so, so bright. *Peaceful.*

JOHN *looks around, then picks up the razor. Places it in* JULIE*'s hands. He goes to her. Whispering:*

JOHN Go then. Here's your broom. Go, now that it's light out . . . to the barn and . . .

JOHN *whispers in her ear—he is so frightened now. Near tears.* JULIE, *however, is almost smiling. She closes her eyes.*

JULIE . . . yes. Thank you. I'm going now, to my rest. (*Beat.*) But tell me one thing, just before I . . . tell me that it's possible for the first to also receive God's grace . . . Say it. Even if you don't believe it.

JOHN "The first?" No, I . . . I *can't*, Miss! I'm not able to because I don't think that it's true.

JULIE . . . *John* . . .

JOHN I can tell you this, though . . . you're no longer one of the first . . . I'm sure of it. You're one of the very last now . . .

JULIE I *am*! I'm the very last one! (*Turning to the stairs.*) But I can't go now! I *can't*! (*To* JOHN.) Tell me one more time . . . just tell me what to do!

JOHN I can't! I can't, Miss!

JULIE Tell me!

JOHN I CAN'T! JUST GO! PLEASE! GO NOW!!

The bell rings again. Two short bursts. They both look up at it. Terrified.
JOHN *kisses her, holds her tight. Then he turns her toward the stairs and*
pushes her along.

JOHN Don't think! Don't think about it! Just go!!

JOHN *is moving* JULIE *toward the stairs. Helping her on her way out. He*
speaks as they go:

JOHN It's taking my strength away . . . getting weak . . . it's that *bell*!!
I'm afraid of a *bell*! But it isn't just a bell, there's someone behind
it! A hand that's setting it in motion! And it'll just keep ringing and
ringing and ringing, no matter what I do!! Cover my ears or run
and hide, it doesn't matter! It keeps ringing!! He just rings it and
rings it, louder and longer and louder!! And if I don't answer it,
then he'll ring the police, and then . . . and then it'll be too late!
TOO LATE FOR US! IT'S TOO LATE!

The bell rings again. Loud blasts. They both look over at it. JOHN
is losing his courage fast. JULIE *reaches out to touch his cheek.*

JOHN Go now . . . it's horrible but there's no other way . . . you have
to . . . *Go. GO!!*

JOHN *kisses her hand, burying his face in it. Trying to gather strength*
from her. She smiles at him through her tears. She nods and turns,
walking up and out.

JULIE . . . and the first shall be last . . .

JULIE *gets swallowed up in a shaft of blazing sunlight.* JOHN *looks around, paralyzed with fear. Unsure what to do next.*

The bell rings again. Two sharp shocks of electricity. JOHN *moves quickly to the table and starts gathering up the money that has fallen to the floor in his haste. He stuffs it back into the purse but there is still more to be gathered.*

Fluttering bills that are just out of reach. JOHN *crawls around on the floor like an animal, trying to gather up the rest of the money.*

The bells ring again. He looks up with wild eyes. He gets back down and scurries on his hands and knees. Trying in vain to hide his crimes from the world around him.

The bells continue to ring. Again and again.

A song from the period begins to softly play. Something like Annette Hanshaw singing "Wasting My Love On You."

The lights slowly fade until nothing but shadows remain.

Projection #4: "Miss Julie." (Blood red.)

Silence. Darkness.